Visegrad Studies on Americas
Past and Present

Visegrad Studies on Americas
Past and Present

EDS.
ANNA BARTNIK
AGNIESZKA MAŁEK

Cracow 2016

Reviewer
dr hab. Paweł Laidler, prof. UJ

Editing
Anna Sekułowicz

Cover design
Paweł Sepielak

Publication of this volume was financially supported
by the Faculty of International and Political Studies,
Institute of American Studies and Polish Diaspora,
and the "Bratniak" Students' and Graduates'
of Jagiellonian University Foundation

ISBN 978-83-7638-785-7

KSIĘGARNIA AKADEMICKA
ul. św. Anny 6, 31-008 Cracow
tel./faks: 12 431 27 43, 12 421 13 87
e-mail: akademicka@akademicka.pl
Internet bookshop: www.akademicka.pl

Contents

Contents

Preface

The origins of this book are to be found in the wish to promote and enhance cooperation between scholars from Visegrad countries: the Czech
Republic, Hungary, Poland and Slovakia. In spite of significant interest
in American Studies in each country, there has so far been no regular cooperation among scholars, researchers and students. Therefore, we invited
authors representing various disciplines relating to American studies to
join us in an attempt to integrate scholars and create an academic space
for future projects and educational programs. This volume is a consciously
interdisciplinary exploration of contemporary America. Although we have
tried to expand the traditional perspective on the notion of American
studies, too often limited to the United States, to include southern parts
of the continent, the preponderance of research on the US has proven
fairly enduring. Despite this, we are convinced that the collection reflects
the main features of the field of American studies as well as research and
teaching interests and expertise of its practitioners in Visegrad countries.
The texts have been chosen for their relevance to understanding American
social, political and cultural life. At the same time, we are aware of certain omissions in this volume (to name just one example: the formation
of American studies in the Czech Republic). We also realize that Latin
America is underrepresented in the book. In our efforts to collect the
most representative team of authors and research areas, Latin Americanists
from Visegrad countries appeared to be little responsive. The collection,

however, is aimed at being the first step towards broader, long-term and fruitful academic collaboration and hopefully this and other topics will be tackled in the subsequent volume(s). We hope that this volume proves useful for students in the whole range of social and cultural studies as well as for those who share an interest in American society.

The content of the book is not divided into certain sections, but at least three leading themes can be indicated. The authors whose articles are included in the first part examine national and/or local developments in the field and various experiences and paths towards the institutionalization of American Studies in their countries. Their efforts aim to show the state of American Studies on Visegrad's educational map. Radosław Rybkowski introduces the conditions under which American studies emerged in Poland. Réka M. Cristian provides an overview of the history of American studies in Hungary. She points out a specific subversive role which this field played within Hungarian higher education during the Cold War period. In the third chapter, somewhat autobiographical, Peter Rusiňák argues that American studies cannot be limited to traditional subjects such as literature, languages and social and political science, but need a gradual shift towards business-oriented themes. In his view such a change is necessary in order to respond to local and global market needs.

The second section focuses on social and political issues: foreign policy, political rhetoric, migration, citizenship. Ewelina Gutowska-Kozielska analyzes the rhetoric used by Rush Limbaugh, radio talk show host, political commentator and one of the most influential figures among conservative audiences. In her article, the author focuses in particular on Limbaugh's rhetoric about Hillary Clinton, arguing that the techniques he uses and the words he chooses to describe Clinton's behavior and actions result in a construction of reality in which Clinton is the enemy of Republican ideals and values and should not be a part of the American political landscape. Jan Bečka and Maxim Kucer examine the so called American 'pivot to Asia', i.e. the strategic shift towards the Asia-Pacific region announced by Hillary Clinton and Barack Obama in 2011. The authors ask whether the 21st century will be a 'Pacific century' for the US and whether this will enable the United States to decrease its commitment to Europe. Beatrix Balogh provides an overview of the politics of citizenship in US Territories and examines recent trends and events that can influence the current academic debate and transform it into an agenda-setting issue. Anna Bartnik highlights selected issues related to illegal immigration in the US and focuses on differences between words or phrases used to describe the unauthorized immigrant population. Emőke Horváth discusses church-state relations in Cuba in the post-revolutionary years and explores the factors that caused more than 130 priests to leave the island in 1961. William R. Glass analyzes the evolution of the way that westerns (and especially a subgenre called by the author 'Americans in Mexico') depicted a growing disillusionment with US foreign policy of intervention designed to promote independence and economic development in the first two decades of the Cold War.

The last part of the book focuses on music, literature and theatre and addresses the question of faith, collective memory and identity, which is discussed from a cultural perspective. Krisztina Magyar explores conceptualization of the Church of England as a mother in four documents compiled in the 17th century by two prominent Puritan preachers, John Cotton and Richard Mather. Irén Annus focuses on the role of humor in religion. Although the author generally agrees with the quote "Humor and religion are not the best of friends", she takes a closer look at the Jane Austen adaptation entitled *Pride and Prejudice: A Latter-day Comedy* (2003) and explores the role of humor in Mormonism. Orsolya Anna Sudár presents the significant role of collective memory. Societies need continuity and connection with the past for their coherent development. The author analyzes two occurrences, the Triangle Shirtwaist Factory fire of 1911 and the first bombing of Wall Street on September 16, 1920, to show the relation between the visual documentation, representation and expectations of urban trauma. Ivan Lacko analyzes the approach that Suzan-Lori Parks takes in *The America Play* to challenge the framing of African American history, culture, politics and language, and discusses the intricacies of the consequent reframing of these terms.

This book would not be possible without the help and encouragement of several people. We would like to thank all the contributors for their work and patience with the editing process. We are very grateful to Professor Paweł Laidler for his helpful comments and suggestions for improvement. The Faculty of International and Political Studies and the Institute of American Studies and Polish Diaspora of the Jagiellonian University provided necessary financial support that made the project possible. We would like to thank the above institutions, and especially Prof. Adam Walaszek and Prof. Adam Krzanowski for their generosity. We are also grateful for financial help received from the "Bratniak" Students' and Graduates' of Jagiellonian University Foundation. Last but not least, our gratitude extends to our colleagues who devoted their precious time to read and comment on the articles.

Anna Bartnik and Agnieszka Małek

Radosław Rybkowski

Across the Atlantic

Why American Studies in Poland?

Significant Polish-American encounters (apart from colonial times) began during the American Revolution. Two heroes of the fight for independence: Casimir Pulaski and Thaddeus Kosciuszko were praised on both sides of the Atlantic. The latter in particular has his place in the history of both the United States (as the officer that set grounds for the West Point academy) and Poland (as the leader of the so-called Kosciuszko Insurgency of 1795) (Burczak; Pula; Fried). The role of Thaddeus Kosciuszko was marked by the letters he exchanged with some of the Founding Fathers, including Thomas Jefferson and James Madison. The letters that can still be accessed in the Czartoryski Library of the Polish National Museum in Krakow (Storozynski).

The ties between Poland and the United States, or rather between Poles and America, became even closer due to the mass migration of the 19th and early 20th century. Hundreds of thousands of people from then partitioned Poland moved to the United States looking for political freedom and/or economic prosperity (Walaszek). This mass migration could not remain without some impact on the growing interest among Poles in American culture, society, history, literature, etc. One of the prominent examples of such a shift was the collection of short stories written by Henryk Sienkiewicz (the future Nobel laureate in literature), describing the not-so-bright life on the other side of the Atlantic, in e.g. *Sachem* or *A Memory of Mariposa* (Sienkiewicz 1973).

But it was the beginning of the 20th century that saw the first Polish-American intellectual encounter. Poland, regaining its independence, with more than one million Poles living in the United States, had to make an effort to understand the people and the country that achieved such power and which had long advocated for Polish full sovereignty. One of the first persons to provide a deeper insight into American culture was Roman Dyboski, for many years Chair of English Literature of the Jagiellonian University in Krakow (Prezydent R.P. 1921; 1936). He went to the United States to popularize knowledge about Poland and its cultural achievements, but during his stay he also explored American literature, resulting not only in the first Polish academic book in this field, but also in many other publications on the United States (Dyboski 1930a; 1930b; 1930c; 1932a; 1932b).

The economic expansion of the USA and its growing cultural prominence was also reflected in popular culture. Jazz music and Hollywood film productions became familiar not only to Polish cultural elites. The advancements of technology (film, radio, and gramophone) made American culture widely accessible and consumed by Polish society. Both highbrow and lowbrow US art became admired by some and at the same time criticized by others, as an example of the decline of Western civilization. The tragic events of World War II brutally cut off our growing mutual interest. The post-war communist takeover and the Iron Curtain brought cultural relations and academic research on the United States to a sudden stop. Even the Fulbright education program in Poland initiated in 1959 emphasized research cooperation rather than mutual cultural understanding (Polish-American Fulbright Commission).

The times of the Cold War called for profound knowledge of the opponent, which was the reason of the emergence of Sovietology as a new field of studies in the United States. The Polish government in the 1970s was also looking for the opportunity to promote research on the United States. Thanks to the activity of Professor Andrzej Bartnicki, with the support of both the Polish government and the United States Information Agency, a formal agreement between University of Warsaw and University of Indiana, Bloomington was signed. Thus, in 1976, the American Studies Center (ASC) of the University of Warsaw opened its doors. At first, the ASC was an institution focusing only on research and offering no formal program of studies (Michałek).

A little earlier, in 1972, another research-oriented institution was established in Kraków: the Institute of the Polish Diaspora of the Jagiellonian University. Although focused on the problems of Polish migration to other countries and the Polish diaspora, right from the very start it had very close connections with American scholarship and American Studies. The reason was fairly obvious: on the one hand, the most advanced research on migration was conducted in the United States; and on the other, the largest and most important Polish diaspora lived in the United States (Miodunka). Therefore, researchers working at the Institute of the Polish Diaspora also investigated such issues as race and color in the USA; history of the US press or history of amateur theatre in the US.

Political transformation in Central and Eastern Europe changed the situation of American Studies in Poland completely. Firstly, research interest in the United States was no longer a cause for suspicion, but rather the opposite: it was praised as a way of investigating effective solutions for political and economic challenges. Secondly, wider availability of higher education in Poland resulted in a radical increase of student enrollment from just 400,000 in 1990 to almost 2,000,000 in 2004, thus making the space for new programs of studies, and thereby leading to the third important change: in 1996 the American Studies Center launched their structured academic program of studies. In 2001, the Chair of American Studies of the newly established Faculty of International and Political Studies of the Jagiellonian University was the second to start its own M.A. program in American Studies (Faculty of International and Political Studies).

The beginnings of these two institutions, namely the American Studies Center of the University of Warsaw and the Chair of American Studies (now expanded into the Institute of American Studies and Polish Diaspora) of the Jagiellonian University reflect specific features of American Studies as a field of study in Poland. Unlike in many other European countries, the Polish approach to American Studies is not deeply rooted in studying American literature. The founding father of the ASC, Professor Andrzej Bartnicki, was a historian focusing in his research on the role of the United States on the global stage. The man who was responsible for the establishment of the Chair of American Studies in Kraków, Professor Andrzej Mania, is also a historian, mostly interested in US foreign policy and the history of political institutions (Michałek).

The Institute of American Studies and Polish Diaspora of the Jagiellonian University features one key characteristics: it combines not only "classic" American Studies, understood as the research on the United States of America. Equally important is studying Latin American history, politics, and culture, organized around the Chair of Latin America. Thus, the students and the scholars gain much broader perspective that helps to understand dynamics of modern North and Latin America.

American Studies centers everywhere are proud of their interdisciplinary approach. This seems to be an indispensable characteristic of this continuously evolving field of academic inquiry (Campbell and Kean). However, unlike in many European countries, the early development of American Studies in Poland is more closely connected with history or political science than with literature studies. This has enabled Polish Americanists to make interdisciplinarity our common method. Even the specializations in American Studies offered at the institutes of English literature/philology provide a deeper insight into the political history of the United States, the US legal system, the US mass media or the US economy.

The three Polish academic journals in the field of American Studies: *Polish Journal of American Studies* (published by the Polish Association of American Studies); *Ad Americam. Journal of American Studies* (published by the Institute of American Studies and Polish Diaspora), and *The Americanist. Warsaw Journal for the Study of the United States* (published by the American Studies Center) are the perfect proof that after so many years of academic activity it is still impossible to delineate clear borders of the field. Scholars of American Studies in Poland are constantly seeking new inspiring concepts and topics to be investigated. We, *the Americanists*, are of course still eager to interact with colleagues from Europe and the United States, looking for more sophisticated and efficient methods of inquiry. The social and political changes and challenges in the United States still attract new generations of students and scholars ready to look for new questions about America and to question the old answers.

REFERENCES:

Burczak, Michał. "The Creation of an Enduring Legend of the National Hero: A Comparison of Tadeusz Kościuszko and George Washington." *The Polish Review* 59.3 (2014): 25-39. Print.

Campbell, Neil and Alasdair Kean. *American Cultural Studies. An Introduction to American Culture*. New York: Routledge, 2006. Print.

Dyboski, Roman. "Ameryka a Powstanie Listopadowe." *Czas*, no. 276 (1930a). Print.

—. *Amerykanizm*. Warszawa: Drukarnia Koziańskich, 1932a. Print.

—. *Cywilizacja amerykańska a cywilizacja europejska*. Warszawa: n.p., 1932b. Print.

—. "O demokracji amerykańskiej." *Przegląd Współczesny* 95 (1930b): 361-382. Print.

—. *Stany Zjednoczone Ameryki Północnej. Wrażenia i refleksje*. Lwów: Książnica-Atlas, 1930c. Print.

Fried, Daniel. "Poland, America, and the Arc of History." *The Polish Review* 54.2 (2009): 141-146. Print.

History. Faculty of International and Political Studies, n.d. Web. 10 June 2016.

History. Polish-American Fulbright Commission, n.d. Web. 10 June 2016.

Michałek, Krzysztof. "Andrzej Bartnicki (25 czerwca 1933 – 16 marca 2004)." *Rocznik Mazowiecki* 15 (2005): 11-17. Print.

Miodunka, Władysław. *Stan badań nad Polonią i Polakami w świecie*. Warszawa: Kancelaria Sejmu, Biuro Studiów i Ekspertyz, 1998. Print.

Prezydent R.P. "Zarządzenie Prezydenta R.P. z dnia 4 lutego 1921 r." *Monitor Polski* no. 260, poz. 351 (1921). Print.

Prezydent R.P. "Zarządzenie Prezydenta R.P. z dnia 11 listopada 1936 r." *Monitor Polski* no. 263, poz. 464 (1936). Print.

Pula, James S. "Tadeusz Kościuszko: A Case Study in Constructed Historical Symbolism." *The Polish Review* 53.2 (2008): 159-182. Print.

Sienkiewicz, Henryk. *Western Septet. Seven Stories of the American West*. Trans. Marion Moore Coleman. Cheshire: Cherry Hill Books, 1973. Print.

Storozynski, Alex. *Kościuszko. Książę chłopów*. Warszawa: Wydawnictwo AB, 2011. Print.

Walaszek, Adam. *Migracje Europejczyków*. Kraków: Wydawnictwo Uniwersytetu Jagiellońskiego, 2007. Print.

RÉKA M. CRISTIAN

Mapping and Remapping America(s): Perspectives on Hungarian American Studies[1]

American studies in Hungary, similarly to its sibling varieties throughout East-Central Europe, played a special role during the period of the Cold War. The discipline, as Enikő Bollobás writes in "Dangerous Liaisons: Politics and Epistemology in Post-Cold War American Studies", was considered a "subversive field" of study, while its research and teaching in Hungary was seen as a "subversive enterprise" (Bollobás 563). Nevertheless, most East-Central European scholars of American studies did "verify – in a post-communist and post-Cold War environment – the existence of an American Civilization by 'importing America (to pun on Richard Horowitz's expression)' into their own culture" becoming thus "instrumental in the *kind* of civilization they *produce[d]*" (Bollobás 577) by disseminating "advanced ideas in an intellectual environment that did not itself produce them" while testing them in given "historical, social, and cultural contexts" (Bollobás 578).

Hungarian American studies as a more or less unified field of study started with the pioneering work of László Országh (1907-1984). As Zoltán Abádi-Nagy points out, Országh was the author of several innovative books,

[1] This text is an abridged and updated version of my "Introduction. The Road Now Taken: Cultural Vistas in American Studies" chapter from *Cultural Vistas and Sites of Identity: Literature, Film and American Studies* (Szeged: AMERICANA e-BOOKS, 2011).

among them, *Az amerikai irodalomtörténetírás fejlődése* [*The Evolution of American Literary History*] published in 1935 and the first comprehensive history of American literature published in Hungarian entitled *Az amerikai irodalom története* [*The History of American Literature*] (1967), alongside the first introduction to American studies in Hungary, *Bevezetés az amerikanisztikába* [*Introduction to American Studies*] (1972) (Abádi-Nagy b 15). Furthermore, Országh founded the prestigious journal *Hungarian Studies in English* (*HSE*), which he edited between 1963 and 1973. During the 1960s, a pioneer in higher education, too, Országh launched American studies in the Hungarian university system at Lajos Kossuth University, the predecessor of the University of Debrecen and today the host of the North American Department of the Institute of English and American Studies, which is, according to its website, the first to gain accreditation for a Ph.D. program in American Studies (1993) and the first to have its accredited MA program in North American Studies (2008).[2] Between 1989 and 1993, Hungarian English and American studies went through what Abádi-Nagy called the "early-phase-post-communist" period of development, followed by a "post-early-phase post-communist" period (Abádi-Nagy b 13), which ended in 1999 with Hungary's adhering to the Bologna Process, which has been in practice in our higher education starting from 2006.

For many years, American studies in Hungary was considered an offspring of the overall field of English Studies. The first phase of the institutionalization of American studies in our country consisted in scattered attempts made by various English Departments to introduce a more focused research and teaching of topics and fields relating to the United States, especially American literature. Among the professors who conceived and devised the terrain for such emerging American studies programs and departments at Hungarian universities and colleges were László Országh, Sarolta Kretzoi-Valkay, Péter Egri, Zoltán Abádi-Nagy, Zsolt Virágos, Lehel Vadon, Bálint Rozsnyai, Zoltán Kövecses, Tibor Frank and Enikő Bollobás.

With the collapse of communism in 1990 in Hungary, the field acquired a new momentum with Hungarian higher education witnessing

---

[2] See http://ieas.unideb.hu/index.php?p=92.

a much-welcomed proliferation of American studies departments. For example, the Department of American Studies of Eötvös Loránd University in Budapest, currently part of the School of English and American Studies, was founded as an independent program already in 1990 and received academic accreditation four years later, in 1994.[3] This is how Enikő Bollobás writes about the birth of this department:

> One day in the fall of 1989, I received a phone call from Zoltán [Kövecses]: let's set up, now, that department of American studies we have talked about for so long. Indeed, for over a decade we had wanted a separate department for "teaching America," but in Kádár's Hungary the US could only be discussed, at the most, in a colonial manner, as a corner of the English world. The idea of teaching disciplines directly relating to the US and within a separate administrative entity was still anathema: it was considered a subversive act, a revolt against the established order – somewhat like America itself. Charlotte Kretzoi deserves to be remembered as a long time instigator. But I also recall a lunch in 1980 or 1981, for example, which we had in the old cafeteria of the Pesti Barnabás building of ELTE: Zoltán Kövecses, Tibor Frank, and I were trying to talk the then head of the English Department into accepting the possibility of establishing a separate branch of American studies at least within the English Department. I remember well his facial features as he uttered the official verdict with absolute conviction: "no way." Then there were other serious but failed attempts pursued by Charlotte Kretzoi and Tibor Frank through the 80s. The ultimate founding of the department had to wait for the new winds of political change: this is what Zoltán sensed in the fall of that *annus mirabilis* of 1989, prompting him to make his phone call. The two of us sat down to discuss the possibilities and prepare the whole packet for the launching of a new department: documents, proposals, curricula, syllabi, book lists, etc. Then Gyula Kodolányi, long-time member of the English Department, entered and brought along his familiarity with not just American literature, but the new political scene too. Tibor Frank was also brought in, though for the moment only through the telephone, unsure yet as to when he would return after years of teaching in the US It was clear during that historic spring of 1990 that the political changes now allowed, for the first time ever, for the launch-

---

[3] See http://das.elte.hu/.

ing of a separate academic unit for the teaching of American studies. The three of us, Kövecses, Kodolányi, and I, made the necessary visits to government and university administrators, requested the support of the Ministry of Culture (then Deputy Minister Károly Manherz was especially helpful), the Soros Foundation, and USIS, and pinned them down with all the details. By the summer it all came together, and the members of a veritable department were lined up: Zoltán Kövecses, Gyula Kodolányi, Tibor Frank, Enikő Bollobás, Éva Federmayer (with Zsófia Bán, Tamás Magyarics, and Erzsébet Mészáros to join a year later), and two positions for native American language instructors were secured. ELTE's Department of American Studies, the first such full-fledged department in the country, was officially launched in June 1990, with the backing of the new government of József Antall, the Soros Foundation, and the US Embassy. It was only natural that our combative initiator, Zoltán Kövecses, would be its first chair (1990-92). (Bollobás 9-10)

Moreover, the American Studies Department of Károly Eszterházy College in Eger[4] was also founded in the same year as the Department of American Studies of Eötvös Loránd University in Budapest (Abádi--Nagy b 17).

The Department of American Studies of the University of Szeged was also the product of the departmental boom of the early 1990s, with its American studies program launched in the mid-1980s after the European Association of American Studies organized its biennial conference for the first time in a communist country, in Budapest (Rozsnyai). The American studies in Szeged was for a while an independent program of study that emerged later as a Department of American Studies, which is now part of the Institute of English and American Studies of the University of Szeged (http://amerikanisztika.ieas-szeged.hu/). Besides the departments mentioned above, a selection of courses with American topics are currently taught at other universities and colleges, too, in Budapest, Pécs, Veszprém, Nyíregyháza and Szombathely.

Paraphrasing what Clifford Geertz wrote in *The Interpretation of Cultures*, if one wants to understand what American studies in Hungary is, one needs to look not only at its theories, its findings and institutions

---

[4] See http://www.ektf.hu/~amerikanisztika/.

but also at what the practitioners of it do. In this regard, the widening spectrum of research topics and courses at the American Studies Departments and institute of English and American Studies across the country can best describe the current state of the discipline through the interest and work of their faculty.[5]

Periodicals, conferences, as well as other, various publications have played an essential role in the context of the field's institutionalization. The leading journal of English and American studies in Hungary entitled *Hungarian Journal of English and American Studies* (*HJEAS*) published since 1995 by the Institute of English and American Studies, University of Debrecen, evolved out of the *Hungarian Studies in English* (*HSE*, first published in 1963) that was "the only undisrupted periodical sequence devoted exclusively to English and American Studies" in the country, while its successor, *HJEAS*, became "the senior Central European journal of English and American Studies" with issues determined to "respond to the new situation created in the wake of the vast social changes that took place in 1989 in Hungary" (Abádi-Nagy a). In a comprehensive 2005 survey of contemporary journal publishing in American studies, Paul Giles and R. J. Ellis emphasized that *HJEAS* has "deliberately exploited its liminal geographical positions between Eastern and Western Europe"

---

[5] Without any claim to completeness, the current list of Hungarian Americanists includes following professors and researchers: Enikő Bollobás, Vera Benczik, Zsófia Bán, Réka Benczés, Éve Federmayer, Tibor Frank, Zoltán Kövecses, Tamás Magyarics, and Éva Eszter Szabó from Eötvös Loránd, University Department of American Studies; Zoltán Abádi-Nagy, Zsolt Virágos, Tibor Glant, Gabriella Tóthné Espák, Lenke Németh, Gabriella Varró, Judit Molnár, Imola Bülgözdi, Péter Csató, Éva Máthey, Judit Szatmáry, Balázs Venkovits, Gergely Máté Balogh, Erika Mikó, and Donald E. Morse from the North American Department, Institute of English and American Studies, University of Debrecen; Lehel Vadon, Judit Szatmáry, András Tarnócz, Judit Kádár, Zoltán Peterecz, Lilla Gyarmati, Renáta Zsámba, Barna Szamosi from the American Studies Department, Eszterházy Károly College in Eger; Károly Pintér, Ildikó Limpár, and Márta Pellérdi from Pázmány Péter Catholic University, Institute of English and American Studies; Gabriella Vöő and Norbert Gyuris from the Department of English Literatures and Cultures, University of Pécs; Irén Annus, Ágnes Zsófia Kovács, Zsófia Anna Tóth, Zoltán Vajda, Zoltán Dragon, and Réka M. Cristian from the American Studies Department, Institute of English and American Studies, University of Szeged; alongside many young researchers pursuing their Ph.D. studies in American topics at various accredited doctoral schools.

becoming a crucial publication articulating many important "counter-narratives on behalf of not just Hungary but Central Europe more generally" (1046). The *HJEAS* and the conference proceedings issued by the HUSSE (Hungarian Society for the Study of English) are the main sites of publications in the field alongside an increasing number of a widening spectrum of topics related to American studies featured in a number of other important Hungarian periodicals, mentioned by Abádi-Nagy in his 2009 survey of the state of the discipline in Hungary. These are the following: the *Eger Journal of American Studies* (published by Károly Eszterházy Teacher's Training College), *Epona* and *Focus* (University of Pécs), *Papers in English and American Studies* (University of Szeged), *Pázmány Papers in English and American Studies* (Pázmány Péter Catholic University), *Studies in English and American* and *The AnaChronist* (Eötvös Loránd University) (Abádi-Nagy b 20-21), among a plethora of books published in both English and Hungarian on American topics. Besides publications, the Hungarian Association for American Studies (HAAS), aiming to advance the study of the United States in Hungary (see http://haashungary.btk.pte.hu/) and currently with a considerable number of members from the above departments and programs, was established in 1992 and has been an active member of the European Association for American Studies (EAAS) since 1994, organizing biannual American Studies conferences in different Hungarian academic venues.

Since its outset, the American studies programs in Hungary had particular dynamics in understanding American culture(s) by taking into account various interacting factors. As Bálint Rozsnyai observed ten years ago in the inaugural issue of *AMERICANA E-Journal of American Studies*,

[in] Hungary we have a special understanding of American culture, in the same way as the Poles have their own special understanding of it. The specialty of the understanding is not the product of an essentialist position: rather it is the outcome of an interaction (series of interactions) of various actors – the US is one among them. Hungary and Poland have their particular understanding/interpretation of "America" – in it the (ex) Soviet Union is undoubtedly a significant factor. (2005)

Informed by these particular dynamics and the most current practices of the field, the open access academic, peer reviewed *AMERICANA E-Journal of American Studies in Hungary* published since 2005 by the Department of American Studies, University of Szeged, alongside with its division, *AMERICANA eBooks*, provides a wide digital forum for scholars and students having interest in the field(s) of American studies.[6] The digital publishing project of the Szeged-based *AMERICANA* was established to promote the use of new media in our current practice of American studies and to enhance the participation, together with the existing printed publications of the field in Hungary, in the ongoing current transnational dialogues about the United States and the Americas as well. Furthermore, the 10th English and Spanish bilingual anniversary issue of this online Hungarian American studies journal[7] coincided with the establishment of the Inter-American Research Center by the American Studies Department and the Hispanic Department in 2015[8] which also embraces researchers from various departments of the Faculty of Arts, University of Szeged that are involved into research and teaching topics focusing on the wider area of the Americas.

REFERENCES:

Abádi-Nagy, Zoltán. "Editorial Note." *Hungarian Journal of English and American Studies*. 1.1 (1995). Web. 13 Oct. 2012. http://dragon.unideb.hu/~hjeas/history.html.
— b. "Anglisztika-amerikanisztika a mai Magyarországon." In: *Anglisztika és amerikanisztika. Magyar kutatások az ezredfordulón*. Eds. Frank Tibor and Károly Krisztina. Budapest: Tinta, 2009: 13-31. Print.
Bollobás, Enikő. "Dangerous Liaisons: Politics and Epistemology in Post-Cold War American Studies." *American Quarterly*, 54.4 (December 2002): 563-579. Print.

---

[6] See http://americanaejournal.hu/ and see http://ebooks.americanaejournal.hu/books/.

[7] See http://americanaejournal.hu/vol11no1.

[8] See http://centro.interamerican.hu/en/.

—. "The Metaphors of Sixty." In: *The Metaphors of Sixty*. Eds. Réka Benczes and Szilvia Csábi. Budapest: ELTE, 2006: 9-11. Print.

Giles, Paul and R. J. Ellis. "E Pluribus Multitudinum: The New World of Journal Publishing in American Studies." *American Quarterly*, 57.4 (December 2005): 1033-1078. Print.

Rozsnyai, Bálint. "Twenty Years of American Studies in Szeged, Hungary." *AMERICANA e-Journal of American Studies in Hungary*. 1.1 (Fall 2005). Web. 21 Sep. 2015. http://primus.arts.u-szeged.hu/american/americana/vol1no1/rozsnyai.htm.

PETER RUSIŇÁK

From Hardware to Soft Skills – North American Area Studies in Slovakia

A View from Bratislavian Center for North American Studies Experience

American Studies, or *Amerikanistika*, as we say in Slovak, has traditionally been represented amongst the academic offer to future university students across various Slovak higher education institutions and their study programs. In fact, this slightly veiled entitlement has been attracting attention of numerous generations of students seeking their degree in a prospective discipline. Furthermore, *Amerikanistika depicts the American dream – bright future with a dream job, work-life balance in the most prosperous countries in the world and many more benefits.* Similar thoughts have been striking the minds of students interested in enrolling to mainly Faculties of Arts (Philosophy, Social Studies or Philology) in Slovakia. Unfortunately, they have been surprised by the fact that *Amerikanistika* no longer represents the bright future of a prospective career and that it has been more and more difficult to stay competitive on the EU job market with a degree in American Studies from Slovak universities.

At the Center for North American Studies, University of Economics in Bratislava, we believe the American Studies programs are not dead in the Slovak environment. They only need an upgrade in order to adapt more to local and global markets' needs and to provide a solid foundation for students whose demand to study the fascinating world of *Amerikanistika* has not decreased over time. Just the opposite!

In our understanding, the field of American Studies is no longer limited to literature, languages, social science and humanities. We have decided to shift the way this field is introduced to students and incorporate more of business-oriented elements into the offer. At the end of the day, we are an economic university focused on business and management – why not to take the best out of this discipline, bring more spices of vital importance for businesses and graduates such as soft skills trainings and create a brand new view on area studies of North American[1] region?

Let me take you back in time to 2006, when two 2nd year students of international relations came up with an idea to establish a student-based NGO at the university campus in Bratislava focused on reinforcing the transatlantic link and raising awareness about the relationships between Central-European countries and the US. The idea in fact was not new – the Euroatlantic Center (EAC) was created long time before, in 1999 by the group of enthusiastic university students in central Slovakia in the city of Banská Bystrica. Basically the two of us overtook the idea of a fully functional non-governmental organization supporting students interested in the issue and brought it over to Bratislava. EAC has always served as a bridge between the academic world of students and the professional world of analysts, diplomats and political experts. Throughout the next three years, I dare to say, we set up a pretty high level of organizational support for students of international relations, organized numerous conferences, meetings, institutional visit of professionals to the university campus and managed to embrace dozens of prospective experts.

When the two of us came close to graduation in 2008, the University of Economics had acknowledged our student activities on the campus and offered us a permanent job in developing the university relationships with the North American region. The newly established university-wide department entitled the Center for North American Studies (CNAS) had become a vital part of the broader concept of area studies at our university targeted to supplement the economic and managerial sciences with "lighter" disciplines. My colleague and predecessor Michal, who launched

---

[1] Our current capacities allow us to consider the US and Canada for the area studies of North American region.

his career as the CNAS executive director in 2009, swiftly jumped into the job with 100% strength while I dedicated "only" 90% of my time to it and meanwhile followed the academic path of Ph.D. studies at the same campus.

Ever since 2008, CNAS has traditionally served its main purpose – overseeing the area studies of North America and developing business-academic cooperation with international companies operating on the basis of North American corporate culture. Rather unique to higher education systems in Central Europe, it links above-average students with private businesses, international experts and academics via innovative methods in teaching. During the full previous seven years, CNAS courses were attended by more than 1600 domestic participants and 280 international students partially completing their studies in Slovakia. The CNAS' story is full of twists and turns, but we have always been keen on our most precious asset – the network. CNAS does not fit into the framework of a traditional university department with its own teachers, researchers and a wide range of compulsory courses. So what is it that we do and what makes us special?

Quite often, I dare to say that we are like a bridge between two distant shores – we bridge a deep gap between the world of academia and the business environment. CNAS puts education right where it is supposed to be – at the heart of *active* students. Those students who think critically, those who want to step aside and who strive to hone their entrepreneurial spirit and become the change they want to see in the world. Our business partners are fully aware of the trend and contribute to the bridging by their know-how, time and desire to raise the higher education level in Slovakia. This is no zero sum game – while getting closer to each other, both sides benefit significantly. Today, the Center offers a comprehensive portfolio of courses and extracurricular activities where students can think critically about both accomplishments and problems of contemporary American and Canadian societies. Thanks to the international academic staff, student involvement in instruction and a primary focus on interactive education, applicable knowledge and case studies, the Center has become a recognized educational initiative. Cooperation with the private sector does not only open a door to talents, but also allows companies to participate in building a knowledge-based economy fostering progressive trends in schooling. On the other hand, it also provides the students a chance to benefit from curricula based on real experiences of the corporate sector.

I am proud to note that the birth and growth of the Center for North American Studies is a telling example of transforming ideas into action, converting visions into reality. Former Slovak ambassador to the US and our academic auspices holder, Amb. Martin Bútora, goes even further in stressing that "the original motivation was a combination of discontent and resolution: on the one hand, the dissatisfaction with traditional instructional practices; on the other hand, the determination to change them. From the very beginning, an underlying belief has been ever-present: for a society in transition like Slovakia, the North American experience in doing business, in designing and implementing various public policies, in problem management, in public debates on politics, in activating civil society is useful. The strategy to achieve this aimed at obtaining approval at the University of Economics and simultaneously at building partnerships, searching for allies and partners" (Bútora). From the very beginnings of our quest, the Center has been blessed with some can-do spirit. We turned the "not always rewarding experience" we had had as students into thinking how we could contribute and introduce a slightly different path in education, one that might perhaps serve as an addition to traditional learning. Having the extraordinary chance to work with outstanding people and the support of the university that entrusted young NGO people with establishing a new university department, we have been fully committed to completing the vision the Center has had. A good friend of mine and my predecessor in the executive director's chair explains that "we tried to create an environment where a student wouldn't be eager just to "pass", but rather to stay committed to an environment that would offer opportunities, inspiration and friendship. Launching North American Studies allowed us not only to teach about US and Canadian economy, politics, and culture, but hopefully helped us to expose the students to the spirit and way of thinking in this – in its own way – exceptional region. Having said all this, the most precious element was the friendship that I saw slowly emerging from daily interactions between the lecturers and the students. Friendship that enabled us to lower power distance, to exchange inspiration, to truly perceive and to humbly learn from the students. And if we can believe in what they say, it was a mutual process" (Kovács).

Seven or eight years is quite a long period of time that tested our position and the path set at the very beginning. Establishing a flexible network of business contacts over the years has allowed us to widen the portfolio of our activities and created, in my own understanding, a highly valuable cooperation. CNAS does not only create a favorable environment for private know-how flowing to the university campus, but it directly organizes its own trainings and education sessions for private businesses. I am especially proud of this aspect, as CNAS is not in the position of the sole know-how receiver anymore, but it can generate a value for businesses by its own. Our flagship service in the area of entrepreneurship education and training proudly bears the name the *Entrepreneurship Training Program*. The first corporation entrusting us with the program was O2 Slovakia and I am also thankful for the kind support of the Embassy of the United State of America to the Slovak Republic. Through this program, CNAS has organized eight quarterly training sessions for almost 140 alumni. Young entrepreneurs and company professionals with outstanding ideas and professional skills often lack proper education and experience, especially in communication. The two-day intensive program is aimed at high-potential and start-up community members empowering them with business etiquette, business communication skills and self-branding soft-skills training. The aim of the program is for the participants to be able to present their arguments and ideas better and in a professional manner and establish new professional contacts and benefit from existing networks in a self-confident and effective way. The trainings are led by professional communication coaches and TEDx speakers from California – John Bates and Nathan Gold.

In September 2015, we opened our 8th academic year as the leader in North American area studies and business-academic cooperation in Slovakia. This time, our focus is directed towards fostering the "business" branch of our activities, which precisely correlates with the students' demand for more practically oriented courses, where the power distance would be decreased and more business case studies would constitute the core of the education. Nevertheless, our students are fully aware of the fact they are enrolled in the programs of mostly economic and managerial disciplines where the "business" element is vital for their future career. We have tried to acknowledge the demand and prepared accredited courses focused on corporate issues such as human resources, business ethics, stakeholder relations and PR. Spiced up with on-hands courses focused on soft skills such as leadership capabilities, personal branding, presentation skills or email communication, we also do not forget about the area studies and we offer courses on Canadian political system, US political and economic system or negotiation and conflict resolution in US context. So far, there has been no opportunity for Slovak students to enroll for, let's say, a complete undergraduate program of North American studies leading to bachelor degree.[2] Not to mention such a program with a business element. A long journey is behind us, but an even longer one is ahead. The Center will need dedicated leaders, employees and friends not to stray from its chosen path.[3]

REFERENCES:

Bútora Martin and Michal Kovács, Peter Rusiňák. "Faces of CNAS". Center for North American Studies, University of Economics in Bratislava. Web. 29 Sept. 2015. http://cnas.euba.sk/data/FacesOfCnas_Brochure2013_ v20131208.pdf.

---

[2] Complete list of courses, curricula, extracurricular activities and all details about CNAS is accesible on: cnas.euba.sk.

[3] Peter Rusiňák no longer serves as CNAS director. In summer 2016, after seven years of service, he decided to pursue his career further at the American Chamber of Commerce in Slovakia, but he stays in close touch with CNAS.

Ewelina Gutowska-Kozielska

At War with Hillary

The Constitutive Rhetoric of the Republican Party

> It's the Rush Limbaugh program. Listen for a couple of
> days and you will come to agree with me. Listen for six
> weeks and you will never doubt me. And listen for six
> months and you will think you've always agreed with me
> (Limbaugh 25 Mar. 2015)

This paper is an attempt to examine the rhetoric of the most prominent
figure in the conservative movement today, the leading American conservative radio talk show host who, for a number of Americans, both liberal and
conservative, is the embodiment of the Republican ideology (Wilson 17)
constructing a reality in which Hilary Clinton, the Democrats' candidate
for President is the ultimate enemy of the Republican ideology and values.

The relationship between discourse, ideology and social power is
strong and indissoluble. The rhetoric intent, the coherence and the biased
outlook on the world that the author and the receiver introduce into/infer
from the text, and the text's interpretation are equally essential. Discourse,
therefore, cannot be simply interpreted in terms reflecting the reality, but
as central to its (re)creation and (re)establishment and carrying the power
that reflects the interests of those who speak or write.

The image – and ideology – of any political party is, to a large extent,
produced and represented via discourse and communication; discourse as
meant here includes written and spoken text as well as non-verbal semiotic

messages i.e. photographs, posters, films etc. There are, of course, other forms of reproduction of ideologies, but discourse "plays a prominent role as the preferential site for the explicit, verbal formulation and the persuasive communication of ideological propositions"; discourse is a specific "textual" form of language use in the social context, and its role as the site for the persuasive presentation of particular ideology propositions.

> (...) ideologies are both cognitive and social. They essentially function as the 'interface' between the cognitive representations and processes underlying discourse and action, on the one hand, and the societal position and interests of social groups on the other hand. (...) Ideologies mentally represent the basic social characteristics of the group, such as their identity, tasks, goals, norms, values, position and resources. (van Dijk a 18)

The selection of appropriate/relevant values and establishing the opposition against the Others (Us vs. Them) are fundamental to the construction of ideologies which, in turn, organize, monitor, manage and control their followers' attitudes and behaviors, especially social opinions of the group's members, and influence their personal cognition and the models they form. Social power as meant here is a property of the relationship between social groups/classes/people as social members, its very notion involving the idea of cognitive control by its agents and presupposing the first party's possession of control over cognitive conditions of the second party's actions such as beliefs, opinions, plans and wishes. Social power is typically indirect and exercised via particular kind of mental control. This type of control usually involves various forms of discursive communication, such as persuasion etc. Resources enabling the exercise of power standardly consist of socially valued but uncommon attributes/possessions (e.g.: rank, authority, social status, knowledge, expertise etc.). The control of discourse and its production belongs to the most important components of social authority. The discursive enactment of power is mostly of persuasive nature. That power of discourse is further enhanced by group power relations such as the opposition between the rich and the poor, white and black, men and women, moral and immoral, in general – us vs. them. As Teun A. van Dijk emphasizes any property of discourse that "expresses, establishes, confirms of emphasizes a self-interested group opinion, perspective or position" should be of special interest when analyzing ideology. Discourse structures implemented when (re)creating a reality relevant for a certain ideology – or – political party and establishing the relationships of power exist on various dimensions. Discourse is ideologically controlled via the control of mental models, and ideologies themselves are (re)constructed, (re)established and (re)produced in the same way. Thus the relation between discourse and ideology is indissoluble.

McGee uses the concept of constitutive rhetoric to describe the power and control structures within human societies, and define the relationship between "the leader [and] the people", for the purpose of which relationship members of every society are trained by the means of rhetoric – or to put it more precisely – persuaded – from the moment they are born.

According to Michael McGee the language of politics is not a precise enough locus of analytic attention, and the traditional focus of rhetorical studies on arguments are insufficient and thus a "mistake" while the key to the questions concerning the substance of ideological language, or the source of the persuasive power of political language and its function as a mechanism of social control is the concept of an ideograph. Ideographs epitomize the normative, collective commitments of people and fulfill their functions as the indispensable justifications or motivations for actions committed on behalf of the public. Ideographs as such have no disembodied fundamental meaning – there only exist countless uses of notions/concepts in texts and other discursive performances. McGee described ideographs as "agencies of social control" and "agents of political consciousness" that do not use the classical conditioning and neither operate mechanically; as individuals are conditioned to a vocabulary of concepts whose function is that of "guides, warrants, reasons or excuses for behavior and belief". Ideographs are, then, those recurrent words, labels, or expressions that guide and warrant behavior and belief; a culture's ideographs are its dominant "vocabulary of motives; (…) are the terms we use to impart value, justify decisions, motivate behavior, and debate policy initiatives" (McGee 346).

The constitutive rhetoric of the Republican Party i.e. that of war, of a world where the good and honorable *we* must fight or, perhaps defend *our* lives, homes, and values against *them*, in tune with the political and social views of its supporters, creates a hostile version of reality in which it the Party's existence is indispensable. Republican views concerning concepts such as the position of women in the society and its structure when viewed as rhetorical case studies provide insight into specific formulae applied in order to express dissent of less conservative ideology and to, by means of persuasion into action, change (amend?) the existing world order. Republicans via the media often – consciously or not – attempt at creating ideographs which, triggering the desired reaction, would establish the vision of the world in which representatives of the Democrats, especially female politicians are the ultimate enemy. For many strongly opinionated Republicans Hillary Clinton – the former Secretary of State, the wife of a former American President and the Democrats' candidate for President in 2016 – is that enemy. For them, she, i.e., a woman not feminine enough, squelchy (Limbaugh 10 Apr. 2015), self-confident – seems to be the embodiment of that power of evil and, apparently, it is only a question of the degree of evilness. Hillary herself became an ideograph crucial to the rhetoric of the Republican Party, crucial to the process of conjuring the readers/audience into what its supporters believe to be objective reality. The rhetoric of Rush Limbaugh, a leading radical American entertainer, radio talk show host most popular among conservative audience (TALKERS Magazine Online), a writer, and conservative political commentator, best known for *Rush Limbaugh Show*, described by the White House as "the head of the Republican Party" (Farhi), his theories about liberal bias in the American media and his calls for the adoption of core conservative philosophies in order to ensure the Party's survival, appears instrumental in efforts to create an image of Hillary Clinton as the enemy of *real* America and became, in a way, standardized rhetoric of radical conservatives. The popularity of Limbaugh – the techniques used by Limbaugh – creating the dichotomy between average American citizen and Hillary, the cold and the kind, creating – and popularizing the infamous Republican ideograph – testicle lockbox, the universality of opinions and definitions served one overriding purpose – to result in common acknowledgement of the fact that Hillary Clinton should never be a part of American politics. Limbaugh repeatedly describes Clinton's behavior and actions and – thus – constructs her image – using the rhetoric of war, and, simultaneously speaking from the position of authority, of a teacher or a spiritual guide Limbaugh presents himself as the voice, or, perhaps, the consciousness of the *right* part of the nation always on the lookout for the priorities:

"The truth's the truth. That's all I care about here." (Limbaugh 2 Oct. 2014)

And, recognizing the importance of rhetoric,

> Conservatism – the right things, the right values – is worth defending. Each day when I get up, I see people that I love, and things I believe in under a savage attack by the media, by the Democrat Party and my instinct is to come here and defend it. (Limbaugh 19 Mar. 2015)

He re-establishes his own image as the man of value.

The rhetoric of responsibility on the part of the leader is the introduction to the powerful type of the rhetoric of reification – i.e. that of duty – when the duty is on the target audience. He invites his audience to reconsider their reality, presupposing – they would share his observations and conclusions due to the persuasive nature of the images he presents and the audience's ability to think and analyzes on their own, thus – establishing the bond between himself and the people, a group intellectually superior to other, blind victims of the liberal media. Having established himself as the leader – the authority entitled both to speak on the behalf of and to educate his audience in explicitly persuasive tone Limbaugh explains what needs to be done, preparing the ground for future actions. He uses several techniques to create the image of the enemy:

> She's a phony. There are no coincidences with the Clintons. Nothing just spontaneously happens. Everything is orchestrated, everything is planned, everything is staged (…) her spontaneous road trip in the van is phony. Her unscripted sit-downs with, quote, unquote, 'everyday Americans,' are phony. (…) Her claim to care about everyday Americans is phony, as evidenced by, well, her life. (Limbaugh 13 Feb. 2015)

The message is clear – Limbaugh's choice of vocabulary does not leave any doubt – the enemy cannot be trusted. That message appears repeatedly in a number of Limbaugh's interviews and programs, together with that of Clinton being presented with the ideograph Limbaugh prides in – the testicle lockbox. There are photos of Clinton holding the testicle lockbox, and a nutcracker – as a figure of the former Secretary of State cracking nuts between her thighs. The implementation of such techniques allows the target audience to enjoy the constructed image of Clinton and perceive her as less of a human being.

The ideograph of a butch woman, disrespectful to men and traditional family values, always valid in American conservative culture, serves as an instrument to emphasize the fact that Clinton is not one of *Us* – but a representative of *Them.*

> Mrs. Clinton doesn't want to ride the bus like everybody else rides the bus. She doesn't want to drive her car like everybody drives their car. She doesn't want to fly commercial like everybody else flies commercial. She doesn't want to campaign like everybody else campaigns. She just wants the job. She wants to be anointed, coronated or what have you. (Limbaugh 31 Jul. 2015)

That kind of discourse, especially in the USA where the ideographs of *being real* and *one of us*, being part of the nation are strongly embedded in culture, is bound to influence the personal cognition of the target readers. Limbaugh reduces Clinton to the category of detestable notions: she is not only a *phoney*, power – greedy, unattractive and incompetent but also cold and unkind:

> Mrs. Clinton is too self-conscious for whatever reason. She cannot act. She simply can't pull it off. She can't act friendly. She can't act nice. She can't act real; (…) she just comes across as stone cold. And that's why they want her to act because they want her to be able to abandon that. (Limbaugh 16 Apr. 2015)

Limbaugh's rhetoric appeals both to the values of everyman/everywoman with Clinton just not being the part of the ingroup:

> But when you think you're better than everybody else, you don't want to abandon that, you don't want to be Mr. Everyman. (Limbaugh 16 Apr. 2015)

The negative image of the representative – or – perhaps – the embodiment – of the outgroup is enhanced by a detailed description. Limbaugh's Clinton, the obviously redundant element of the society, not really suitable for any service is a pathetic, cold, unkind, insecure individual, incapable of establishing any positive relationship, lacking authenticity, affection, hypocritical, fond of intellectual dishonesty, obsessed with power which is a method of relieving self-hatred or the feeling of being inadequate. The target audience is warned against the tricks of incendiary rhetoric of Clinton while Limbaugh employs the rhetoric of duty in a form of a repetitive manual to organize the rebellion against Democrats – to summon Conservatives to resist and fight the person who, being the embodiment of the dishonest liberal values is, at the same time unworthy of anyone's respect:

> She doesn't come across as friendly. (…) I mean, we created this whole concept of a testicle lockbox in connection with Mrs. Clinton. I mean, she has that kind of appeal to people. She's -- you fill in the blanks here. (Limbaugh 25 Aug. 2015)

Limbaugh choice of words is his conscious implementation of rhetorical devices used for the most fundamental purpose of rhetoric – i.e. persuasion and converting the target reader, thus, having created the image of Hillary Clinton as the clueless, cold and incompetent politician and unattractive, old and useless woman he further on rids her of any power:
"She's not even to be scared of, she's less than that." (Limbaugh 12 Mar. 2015)
Emphasizing the fact that Clinton's own party fears that:

> (…) Hillary doesn't have the ability to overcome this and the overall image that's being created by this media attack. (Limbaugh 12 Mar. 2015)

Limbaugh frequently emphasizes his lack of understanding of the fact why Republicans fear this woman

> I mean this as honestly as I can say it. I have never been one of these dazzled, impressed, or afraid of Hillary Clinton. (…) Now, afraid? I wouldn't

like it if she got elected, that would alarm me, but I don't mean it in that way. I run into people on our side scared to death of this woman. I've never understood it. Adults that are 65 and 70 years old, Republican consultants are scared to death of this woman. I don't understand it. I don't even understand. What has she done that makes her so fearsome? What has she done that qualifies her? Everything she's done, to me, has been a giant botch. (Limbaugh 10 Apr. 2015)

Limbaugh seems to combine rhetoric of exposing and responsibility to define the enemy and to prove her paradoxically – a threat to the American values and the country itself, someone dishonest and dangerous and at the same time inadequate, incapable of coping with reality. The process itself appears to be not an elaborate one: he operates within a range of the fears, lacks, dreams and desires of a considerable number of individuals and uses them as a fundament to a rhetorical solution. In such a case that solution does not have to constitute a beneficial option for the people – it is sufficient if the leader is capable of creating a rhetorical situation in which the problem is likely to be resolved for the people to accept it willingly – and accept the version of reality in which the Hillary Clinton is, in fact, the embodiment of evil.

References

Dijk, Teun A. van. "Critical Discourse Analysis", 1998. Web. 25 Apr. 2014. http://www.hum.uva.nl/teun/cda.htm.

Dijk, Teun A. van. "Power and the News". In: *Political Communication and Action*. Ed. D. Paletz, Cresskill, NJ: Hampton Press, 1995: 9-36. Print.

Dijk, Teun A. van. "Structures of Discourse and Structures of Power" 1989. Web. 12 May 2011. http://www.discourses.org/download/articles/.

Dijk, Teun A. van. "Discourse, Knowledge and Ideology." In: *Communicating Ideologies. Multidisciplinary Perspectives on Language, Discourse and Social Practice*. Eds. Martin Pütz, JoAnne Neff & Teun A. van Dijk, Frankfurt am Main: Lang, 2004: 5-38. Print.

Farhi, Paul. "Limbaugh's Audience Size? It's Largely Up in the Air." *The Washington Post* 7 Mar. 2009: 11-12. Print.

Fairclough, Norman. *Language and Power*. London: Longman, 1989. Print.

Fairclough, Norman. *Discourse and Social Change*. Cambridge: Polity Press, 1992. Print.

Fiske, John. *Television Culture*. London: Routledge, 1987. Print.

Fowler, Robert and Bob Hodge. "Critical Linguistics." In: *Language and Control*. Eds. Robert Fowler et al. London: Routledge and Keegan Paul, 1979: 185-213. Print.

Limbaugh, Rush. "Pearls of Wisdom." *The Rush Limbaugh Show*. Web. 8 Sep. 2015 http://www.rushlimbaugh.com/daily/2015/03/25/pearls_of_wisdom.

—. "Democrats are Worried about Mrs Clinton." *The Rush Limbaugh Show*. Web. 12 Sep. 2015. http://www.rushlimbaugh.com/daily/2015/03/12/democrats_worried_about_mrs_clinton.

—. "Why do Republicans Fear this Woman?" *The Rush Limbaugh Show*. Web. Web. 10 Sep. 2015. http://www.rushlimbaugh.com/daily/2015/04/10/why_do_republicans_fear_this_woman.

—. "Hillary Might Be in Real Trouble." *The Rush Limbaugh Show*. Web. 10 Sep. 2015. http://www.rushlimbaugh.com/daily/2015/08/12/hillary_might_be_in_real_trouble.

—. "Hillary Plans to Sue Gun Manufacturers." *The Rush Limbaugh Show*. Web. 8 Sep. 2015. http://www.rushlimbaugh.com/daily/2015/10/06/hillary_s_plan_sue_gun_manufacturers.

—. "Hillary Wants a Coronation." *The Rush Limbaugh Show*. Web. 12 Sep. 2015. http://www.rushlimbaugh.com/daily/2015/07/31/hillary_wants_a_coronation.

—. "Libertarian Rush Baby on Hillary's SNL Appearance – and Authenticity." *The Rush Limbaugh Show*. Web. 11 Sep. 2015. http://www.rushlimbaugh.com/daily/2015/10/05/libertarian_rush_baby_on_hillary_s_snl_appearance_and_authenticity.

McGee, Michael. "In Search of 'the People'." In: *Contemporary Rhetorical Theory: A Reader*. Eds. John Lucaites, Celeste Condit, Sally Caudill. New York: Guilford Press, 1999: 341-356. Print.

Pfeffer, Jeffrey. *Managing with Power: Politics and Influence in Organizations*. Boston, Mass.: Harvard Business School Press, 1992. Print.

The Daily Caller. Web. 22 Sep. 2015. http://dailycaller.com/2015/04/16/phony-rush-limbaugh-dismisses-hillary-clintons-everyman-act/#ixzz3o6WJkCzR.

Wilson, John K. *The Most Dangerous Man in America: Rush Limbaugh's Assault on Reason*. New York: St. Martin's Press, 2011. Print.

Jan Bečka, Maxim Kucer

The US Pivot to Asia

Historical Reflection, Current Situation and Perspectives for the Future[1]

> …The Pacific is the ocean of the commerce of the future. Most future wars will be conflicts for commerce. The power that rules the Pacific, therefore, is the power that rules the world. And, with the Philippines, that power is and will forever be the American Republic…
>
> Senator Albert J. Beveridge, 1900 (Beveridge 704)

As the 19th century drew to its close, the eyes of the American statesmen, businessmen and military leaders became more fixed on Asia-Pacific. With the western frontier on the North American continent largely stabilized, the Republic started to look for new frontiers, new markets and – also – for the prestige associated with being a true world power. With much of the Asian territory already divided between the "traditional" colonial powers, the US had to try hard to find its own place in Asia-Pacific. The acquisition of the Philippines from Spain after the War of 1898 gave the supporters of American imperialism exactly what they were looking for – a base in the region which could become the foundation of the future "American empire". For those who saw the future of the US in acquiring a large and

---

[1] As of August 2015. Due to the length of publishing process the article does not refer to the most recent issues connected with discussed problems.

modern navy for both military and commercial purposes, and the naval bases to support it, the Philippines as well as the other island possessions such as Hawaii or Guam were also of fundamental importance. It seemed that the 20th century would be the American "Pacific Century".

This dream never fully materialized, however. The US was deeply involved in Asia-Pacific for most of the 20th century, but this involvement had both its high and low points and especially during and after the Vietnam War, many in the US started to view the American continued power projection in the area with very mixed feelings. The US never ceased to be a major player in the region, but its focus has shifted, especially in certain periods of time, more towards promoting democracy, human rights and regional economic development. Moreover, towards the end of the 20th century, India and especially China began to be more assertive, taking over some of the previously US-held positions.

The official and highly symbolic reaction came in 2011 when the US announced its "pivot to Asia". This move was inspired by many reasons – the Obama Administration wanted to show that unlike President Bush, it cares more about Asia-Pacific and about its traditional allies in the region, especially those in Southeast Asia (SA). Even though the Bush Administration somewhat renewed US interest in SA after 9/11, particularly by deepening security cooperation with countries such as Thailand or Malaysia (Sutter 101-109), its focus remained in the Middle-East, the Persian Gulf and Northeast Asia (Mauzy and Job 629). The anxiety about the "rise of China" also played its role, as well as the feeling that the US should do more to defend its commercial and political interests in Asia in general. And finally, like in the 19th century, the emphasis on the naval power again came to the fore, for example in the works of Robert Kaplan, but also others. Again, it seemed that a new American "Pacific Century" is in the making…

The aim of this article is to analyze, through the scrutiny of the theoretical framework of the US foreign policy towards Asia-Pacific during the two Obama Administrations and the practical steps taken so far, the significance and impact of the "pivot". The focus is placed on two particular areas – the security dimension and the multilateral institutions. While it is too early to analyze any long-lasting effects this initiative might have on the regional balance of power and on securing the US interests, it might still be worthwhile to offer the first evaluation of the steps taken and their perception by the key actors. The entry hypothesis of the authors is that although the "pivot" represents a shift in the US foreign policy, it was taken for more than it was intended to be by some of the European allies of the US as well as some of the Asian states. The extensive media coverage of it has added to this phenomenon. The US as a global power simply decided on a move aimed at restoring a more favorable balance of power in one of the regions of interest to Washington, without necessarily "abandoning" the others or even drastically reducing its presence elsewhere. After all, the events of the last several years – especially the crisis in Ukraine and the rise of Daesh in the Middle East – clearly show that the United States remains deeply interested and involved in both of these regions.

The authors consider the topic under question a distinct and specific component of the US foreign policy, both due to the changed geostrategic balance (the rise of China and India) and also because of the highly particular relationship the US traditionally has towards Asia. For this reason, the method chosen for dealing with the subject was a unique case study as many of the findings would be difficult to generalize. As the "pivot" is still a relatively recent phenomenon, the main sources of information were documents released by the US administration and statements made by the US and other officials. There are indeed scholarly works which deal with individual aspects of the "pivot" but the issue is still waiting for a truly complex, multi-faceted analysis. The authors, however, made use of some of the existing scholarship and incorporated some of the thoughts and predictions of scholars dealing with the US foreign policy in the Asia-Pacific into their work.

THE INITIAL ANNOUNCEMENT OF THE PIVOT AND ITS JUSTIFICATION

In late 2011, the US presented to the world what seemed to be a major foreign policy shift. In an article by the Secretary of State Hillary Clinton published in October 2011, she declared the Asia-Pacific region pivotal for the future of the United States and the world per se. She stated that the region is "eager for our leadership and our business" and stressed the necessity for a strong US commitment in the region's process of building "more mature security and economic architecture" (Clinton).

A month later in a speech to the Australian parliament, Barack Obama underlined Washington's renewed interest in Asia-Pacific by declaring it a "top priority". Obama described the US as a Pacific nation and emphasized that ". . . the United States will play a larger and long-term role in shaping this region and its future . . ." (Remarks By President Obama to the Australian Parliament, White House 17 Nov. 2011). He also outlined eight key elements of the American presence in the Asia-Pacific region:

- strengthening alliances and partnerships;
- engaging in multilateral organizations;
- increasing American military presence;
- cooperative relationship with China and emerging powers such as Indonesia;
- ensuring maritime security;
- advancing environmental protection;
- advancing human rights and democracy;
- advancing free trade and investment (Remarks By President Obama to the Australian Parliament, White House 17 Nov. 2011).

The main focus, however, was put heavily on the military-security cooperation and on trade and investment issues. The often-complicated relations with China were also mentioned, yet in a fashion sufficiently vague to make the Chinese leadership anxious about true American intentions (Congressional Research Service 18). In the wake of the announcement, the European allies of the US started to express their own anxiety about the US "leaving Europe".

THE SECURITY DIMENSION OF THE PIVOT

Principal focus of the "pivot" (or "rebalance", as it later became known) in Asia-Pacific was placed on SA. Unlike Northeast Asia where the US alliance with the two major countries, South Korea and Japan, has deepened and where the US maintains large military contingents, in SA the US footprint has been much less visible in the last years. The Bush Administration's efforts here consisted chiefly of enlisting the support of SA countries in the war on terror, while other issues were largely neglected. Yet, crucial sea-lanes vital for global trade run through the area and particularly the South China Sea is a major geopolitical hotspot.

Right from the outset of the "pivot", Washington had been relatively active. In November 2011, Obama announced a plan to deploy 2,500 Marines to Australia by 2017, the largest US deployment to the country since WWII, and expansion of American military presence beyond traditional allies – Japan and South Korea ("First"). The deployment of troops in Australia, despite its geographical distance from the Asian mainland, was an obvious attempt to shore up the US military presence in Asia-Pacific. Also in November 2011, Hillary Clinton became the first State Secretary to visit Burma since 1955 and travelled to many other SA countries. The US formally joined the East Asian Summit where it received support for its initiatives from almost every major SA country. They acknowledged the US as "an essential stabilizing force as rising powers, principally China but also India, gain influence" (Bader 8). Witnessing Chinese departure from its "peaceful rise" since 2009 and feeling increasingly insecure, SA nations have welcomed Washington as a strategic partner (Christensen). Tensions between the region's "no. 2 power" and its neighbors increased, mostly over traditionally disputed resources-rich territories in the South China Sea. Beijing, therefore, reacted with concern to Washington's initiatives such as the announcement to boost the weak Filipino navy because the Philippines, along with China, Taiwan, Malaysia, Vietnam, and Brunei contest Spratly Islands, a potentially oil-rich area. The US also came to an agreement with Singapore that permits to dock in rotation four American combat ships, another step to bolster its naval presence in the region (Gady).

Reacting further to increasing Chinese assertiveness, at Shangri-la Dialogue the US Defense Secretary Leon Panetta promised that by 2020 the Navy would deploy 60 percent, up from the current 50 percent, of all the naval assets to the Pacific ("The US Rebalance"). A year later, his successor Chuck Hagel announced the Air Force would also allocate 60 percent of its capabilities to Asia-Pacific ("Hagel in Singapore").

Chinese officials interpreted Washington's plans as a way to contain China. One of the strongest Chinese high-level official responses to the US Asia-Pacific strategy so far was the April 2013 Ministry of National Defense white paper. "Some country has strengthened its Asia-Pacific military alliances, expanded its military presence in the region, and frequently makes the situation there tenser," states the paper without explicitly naming the US ("New Situation").

Nevertheless, China was hardly without blame. Over the years Beijing has expanded its military arsenal without always attempting to conceal it. In mid-2013, Chinese warships were sent to patrol the Chinese exclusive economic zone and in October 2013 Beijing's first fleet of nuclear submarines was dispatched as far as Sri Lanka which unsettled Chinese neighbors and prompted India to speed-up rebuilding its own fleet.

After the P-8 incident in the South China Sea in summer 2014, it seemed that the US and China made a significant step to improve their security relationship. In November 2014, presidents Xi and Obama met at so called Sunnylands 2.0 and announced signing of new Memorandums of Understanding (MOU) presented as a way to improve military-to-military relations because it should "reduce the potential for misunderstanding and miscalculation" ("Memorandum" 1). Also, MOUs may even potentially improve relations of China with its neighbors as Beijing seems to have publicly accepted the international rules of behavior which may make it less unpredictable and international waters and airspace adjacent to China safer (Dutton). The number of incidents in the air between the US and China has decreased since but the full effect of the MOUs is still unknown as the long awaited annex on air-to-air safety was completed only in September 2015. Besides, China has not ceased its aggressive behavior towards its neighbors considering, for instance, its seizure of Scarborough Shoal from the Philippines in summer 2015.

MULTILATERAL INSTITUTIONS

Another pillar of Obama's vision of the US-led regional order has been strengthening America's role in the regional multilateral institutions. The presence of high-ranking US officials at important regional multilateral forums boosts Washington's image and gives it an opportunity to discuss important security concerns, reinforce regional cooperation and build bilateral relationships. In 2010 when Vietnam chaired ASEAN, it supported full US membership in the East Asia Summit, which laid foundations for the first ever visit by the Secretary General of the Vietnamese Communist Party Nguyen Phu Trong in Washington in 2015 (Andrews).

The Obama Administration had been actively involved with ASEAN already since 2009 when Secretary Clinton signed the Treaty on Amity and Cooperation, a crucial document which promotes regional peace and stability across SA. It was a much welcomed move after the very reserved stance of the Bush Administration which sent only low-ranking officials to ASEAN meetings. Another positive sign of the US commitment to the organization was the appointment of the first resident ambassador to ASEAN David L. Carden who was later replaced by Nina Hachigian. Her professional background with focus on Asian foreign policy makes her much more suitable for the position than her predecessor. Almost two years in her term so far, Hachigian has been actively participating in a variety of events across the region.

The success of the US in improving ASEAN integration and leadership in the region collides with China's interests towards the organization as well as with the internal disputes between its 10 member states and unevenness of their economic development. The Expanded Economic Engagement was initiated by the US to expand American trade and investment with ASEAN and potentially pave the way that would bring its so-far not included members into Trans-Pacific Partnership (TPP), a high--standard free-trade pact, "[t]he centerpiece of our economic rebalancing", as National Security Adviser Donilon put it in early 2013 ("Remarks by Tom Donilon"). TPP, an American initiative, has been promoted as a major trade deal that would especially boost economies of its Asian members, while the gains would be only modest for the US (Petri and Plummer 6). The TPP negotiations have been extremely difficult, however, and only in October 2015 did the parties involved reach an agreement. The US Congress, however, as well as all the other member states, must still approve the treaty. From the perspective of the US strategic goals in Asia-Pacific and the emphasis it places on region's significance, the consequences of TPP's failure may be rather grim as Obama recognized: "[vewe've got to make sure we're writing those trade rules in the fastest-growing region of the world, the Asia-Pacific, as opposed to having China write those rules for us" ("WSJ Interview"). Although TPP's completion is still a work in progress, Washington did achieve to bring in initially reluctant Japan, which gives the TPP more weight (Goodman and Green).

However, China will be absent from the pact. At first reserved towards TPP, China changed its view to a more favorable one (Ye). Yet, Washington's reluctant and sometimes unfriendly stance towards potential Chinese membership as well as American objectives within the "rebalance" strategy motivated Beijing to put more effort in creating regional integration on its own. "One Belt, One Road" serves as an umbrella term for two large-scale development initiatives, the Silk Road Economic Belt and the Maritime Silk Road, introduced by Xi in 2013, and other projects such as Asian Infrastructure Investment Bank (AIIB), a rival of IMF, founded a year later. Partly, these ambitious initiatives are Beijing's response to American "rebalance" (but on much larger geographical scale connecting Asia, Europe, and Africa), even more so when considering the fact that the US is not, and does not wish to be, a member of AIIB nor of the Regional Comprehensive Economic Partnership (RCEP). Unlike TPP, RCEP's entrance requirements are lower making it, therefore, more inclusive. Thus, the US-backed trade pact maselose some of its relevance if not practically implemented soon.

THE REBALANCING FOUR YEARS ON: "PIVOT TO NOWHERE?" (COLLINSON)

As the end of the second term of the Obama Administration is coming close, the President will be even more eager to leave behind him a legacy, both in the domestic politics and on the international scene. The pivot, or rebalancing to Asia, can be such a legacy in the latter sphere if it brings tangible results. How can we assess the situation so far?

The events on the international scene have taken quite a sharp turn since the pivot's official launch in autumn 2011. US military is once more actively involved in combat operations in Iraq, and now also in Syria, to counter the Islamic State. At the same time, the conflict in Ukraine propelled by Russian involvement there led the US, for instance, to launch the European Reassurance Initiative (ERI) aimed at bolstering the defense capacity especially of Alliance's eastern flank (see "Fact" for more on ERI). The US presence in Europe is also being strengthened again, although largely on rotational basis.

In comparison, the steps taken in Asia-Pacific might seem rather timid at a first glance. However, it does not necessarily mean that the "pivot" has been abandoned. The US at the moment remains the only true global power able to be militarily engaged in two or more operations (on a limited scale) simultaneously. The problem in Asia-Pacific is that unlike in Europe, there is no military pact comparable to NATO. The ASEAN's founding principles make it impossible to become a venue for military cooperation. The US is working with a number of allies and sympathizers that are often united only by their anxiety about the rise of China. In the South China Sea, the countries involved are not united to oppose the Chinese claims – rather they see each other as rivals as well. This is also reflected in the US approach, where the US Asia-Pacific Maritime Security Strategy talks about the need to resolve these disputing claims peacefully and by legal means ("Asia-Pacific Maritime Security Strategy"). It is clear that at the moment Washington is anxious to avoid any exacerbation of tensions in the region and that it hopes to keep China on board.

With regards to the efforts in the area of TPP, the results have been mixed so far and the initiative is well behind schedule. The reason for this is not only the fact that, as already mentioned, the negotiations between the participating countries have been very complex and painful compromises have had to be made by all sides. There also is a potential problem with getting the treaty ratified by the US Congress where it is opposed not only by some Republicans, but also by certain Democrats. There are for example fears that the TPP would lead to job cuts in the United States, which would make it unpopular with the electorate. The President, however, has scored one victory already, when, after a long and complicated battle, he managed to convince the Senate to approve what is called the "fast track authority" – he was authorized to negotiate with the other countries and present to the Congress the final package without having to submit it to amendments and changes from the lawmakers (Lewis). The Congress, however, can of course still reject the treaty and so the result is still uncertain at best.

What can we say in conclusion? The question posed in the beginning was whether it was possible to expect that the US would shift its primary attention on Asia and loosen its commitment to Europe – in other words, whether the 21st century would be a "Pacific Century" for the US. The answer, based on the developments from 2011 to now, is no. At the moment, the US cannot afford to focus solely on any particular region and ignore other ones completely. Washington's interests are global and so is its responsibility. For those that have expected immediate and spectacular results, the "pivot" must be a disappointment so far – the TPP is still long way from being implemented, the US presence in Asia has been strengthened but China was not deterred from its military build-up (Babones). But, in general, compared to some other areas where the US was heavily engaged during the previous years, such as the Middle East, Asia-Pacific remains a "success story". The TPP's eventual success or failure aside, perhaps the most important legacy of the Obama Administration's Asia-Pacific policy will be that no major crisis or confrontation has taken place in the region during his two terms in office and that the US standing and image there have actually improved…

References:

"Asia-Pacific Maritime Security Strategy", US Department of Defense, 14 Sep. 2015. Web 12 Dec. 2015. http://www.defense.gov/Portals/1/Documents/pubs/NDAA%20A-P_Maritime_SecuritY_Strategy-08142015-1300-FINALFORMAT.PDF.

Andrews, Brian. "The Pivot's Legacy: Locking in US Presence and Building Effective Institutions in Asia." National Interest. Center for National Interest, 6 Aug. 2015. Web. 15 Sep. 2015. http://www.nationalinterest.org/blog/the-buzz/the-pivot%E2%80%99s-legacy-locking-us-presence-building-effective-13510.

Babones, Salvatore. "Why China's Massive Military Buildup Is Doomed." National Interest. Center for the National Interest, 5 Aug. 2015. Web. 23 Sep. 2015. http://nationalinterest.org/feature/why-chinas-massive-military-buildup-doomed-13494.

Bader, Jeffrey A. *Obama and China's Rise. An Insider's Account of America's Asia Strategy.* Washington, D.C.: Brookings Institution, 2012. E-book.

Beveridge, Albert J. "In Support of the American Empire". Record, 56th Congress, I Session, 1900: 704-712.

Brzezinski, Ian. "The European Reassurance Initiative's One Year Anniversary: Mixed Results." Atlantic Council. Atlantic Council, 3 Jun. 2015. Web. 24 Sep. 2015. http://www.atlanticcouncil.org/en/blogs/natosource/the-european-reassurance-initiative-s-one-year-anniversary-mixed-results.

Christensen, Thomas J. "The Advantages of an Assertive China." *Foreign Affairs.* 11 Mar. 2011. Web. 10 Aug. 2015. https://www.foreignaffairs.com/articles/east-asia/2011-02-21/advantages-assertive-china.

Clinton, Hillary. "America's Pacific Century." Foreign Policy. Foreign Policy Group. 11 Oct. 2011. Web. 12 Sep. 2015. http://foreignpolicy.com/2011/10/11/americas-pacific-century/.

Collinson, Stephen. "Obama's Pivot to Nowhere." CNN.com. Cable News Network. 16 Jun. 2015. Web. 12 Aug. 2015. http://edition.cnn.com/2015/06/16/politics/obama-trade-china-asia-pivot/.

Congressional Research Service. "Pivot to the Pacific? The Obama's Administration 'Rebalancing' Toward Asia." CRS Report for Congress. 28 Mar. 2012. Web. 29 Aug. 2015. https://www.fas.org/sgp/crs/natsec/R42448.pdf.

Dutton, Peter A. "MOUs: The Secret Sauce to Avoiding a US-China Disaster?" National Interest. Center for National Interest, 30 Jan. 2015. Web. 15 Sep. 2015. http://nationalinterest.org/feature/mous-the-secret-sauce-avoiding-us-china-disaster-12154.

"FACT SHEET: European Reassurance Initiative and Other US Efforts in Support of NATO Allies and Partners." WhiteHouse.gov. White House, 3 Jun. 2014. Web. 14 Sep. 2015. https://www.whitehouse.gov/the-press-office/2014/06/03/fact-sheet-european-reassurance-initiative-and-other-us-efforts-support-.

"First Contingent of 200 US Marines Arrives in Darwin." BBC News. BBC, 12 Apr. 2012. Web. 5 Sep. 2015. http://www.bbc.com/news/world-asia-17606594.

Gady, Franz-Stefan. "4 US Littoral Combat Ships to Operate out of Singapore by 2018." *The Diplomat.* 19 Feb. 2015. Web. 20 Sep. 2015. http://thediplomat.com/2015/02/4-us-littoral-combat-ships-to-operate-out-of-singapore-by-2018/.

Goodman, Matthew P. and Michael J. Green. "Why Japan Should Join the TPP." CSIS. Center for Strategic and International Studies, 10 Mar. 2013. Web. 22 Sep. 2015. http://csis.org/publication/why-japan-should-join-tpp.

"Hagel in Singapore on US Security Policy in Asia-Pacific Region." US Department of State, 3 Jun. 2013. Web. 6 Sep. 2015. http://london.usembassy.gov/forpol415.html.

Hughes, Kristina. "US Hosts Meeting Next Week in Bid to Wrap up Pacific Trade Pact." Reuters. Ed. W. Simon and Ken Willis. Thomson Reuters, 24 Sep. 2015. Web. 30 Sep. 2015. http://www.reuters.com/article/2015/09/25/us-trade-tpp-usa-idUSKCN0RO1UL20150925.

Kaplan, Robert. *Monsoon: The Indian Ocean and the Future of American Power.* New York: Random House, 2010. Print.

Lewis, Paul. "Barack Obama Given 'Fast-track' Authority over Trade Deal Negotiations." *Guardian*, 24 Jun. 2015. Web. 24 Sep. 2015. http://www.theguardian.com/us-news/2015/jun/24/barack-obama-fast-track-trade-deal-tpp-senate.

Mauzy, Diane K. and Brian L. Job. "US Policy in Southeast Asia. Limited Re-engagement after Years of Neglect." *Asia Survey* 47.4 (2007): 622-641. Web. 11 Mar. 2016. http://www.hks.harvard.edu/fs/pnorris/Acrobat/Burma_Mauzy_Job.pdf.

"New Situation, New Challenges and New Missions." Mod.Gov.cn. Ministry of National Defense the People's Republic of China, 13 Apr. 2013. Web. 19 Sep. 2015. http://eng.mod.gov.cn/Database/WhitePapers/2013-04/16/content_4442752.htm.

Petri, Peter A. and Michael G. Plummer. "The Trans-Pacific Partnership and Asia-Pacific Integration: Policy Implications." IIE.com. Peterson Institute for International Economics, 1 Jun. 2012. Web. 17 Aug. 2015. http://www.iie.com/publications/pb/pb12-16.pdf.

"Remarks by National Security Advisor Tom Donilon – As Prepared for Delivery." WhiteHouse.gov. White House, 15 Nov. 2012. Web. 11 Sep. 2015. https://www.whitehouse.gov/the-press-office/2012/11/15/remarks-national-security-advisor-tom-donilon-prepared-delivery.

"Remarks By President Obama to the Australian Parliament." WhiteHouse.gov. White House, 17 Nov. 2011. Web. 5 Sep. 2015. https://www.whitehouse.gov/the-press-office/2011/11/17/remarks-president-obama-australian-parliament.

"Remarks by Tom Donilon, National Security Advisor to the President: The United States and the Asia-Pacific in 2013." WhiteHouse.gov. White House, 10 Mar. 2013. Web. 17 Sep. 2015. https://www.whitehouse.gov/the-press-office/2013/03/11/remarks-tom-donilon-national-security-advisor-president-united-states-an.

Sutter, Robert G. *The United States in Asia*. Lanham, Boulder, New York, Torronto, Plymouth, UK: Rowman & Littlefield Publishers, 2009. E-book.

"The Memorandum of Understanding Between the United States of America Department of Defense and the People's Republic of China Ministry of National Defense on Notification of Major Military Activities Confidence-Building Measures Mechanism." Defense.gov. US Department of Defense. Web. 14 Sep. 2015. http://www.defense.gov/Portals/1/Documents/pubs/141112_MemorandumOfUnderstandingOnNotification.pdf.

"The US Rebalance Towards the Asia-Pacific: Leon Panetta." IISS.org. International Institute for Strategic Studies, 2 June 2012. Web. 6 Sep. 2015. https://www.iiss.org/en/events/shangri%20la%20dialogue/archive/sld12-43d9/first-plenary-session-2749/leon-panetta-d67b.

"US Trade Representative. Preamble." The Trans-Pacific Partnership. A Medium Corporation US. 5 Nov. 2015. Web. 12 Mar. 2016. https://medium.com/the-trans-pacific-partnership/preamble-b408ed30f42c#.knkbvx2u4.

Wallace Cheng, Shuaihua. "China's New Silk Road: Implications for the US." Yale Global Online. Yale U, 28 May 2015. Web. 18 Sep. 2015. http://yaleglobal.yale.edu/content/china%E2%80%99s-new-silk-road-implications-us.

"WSJ Interview Transcript: President Obama on TPP, China, Japan, Pope Francis, Cuba." Blogs.WSJ.com. Dow Jones & Company, 27 Apr. 2015. Web. 13 Aug. 2015. http://blogs.wsj.com/washwire/2015/04/27/wsj-interview-transcript-president-obama-on-tpp-china-japan-pope-francis-cuba/.

Ye, Min. "China Liked TPP – Until US Officials Opened Their Mouths." *Foreign Policy*. 15 May 2015. Web. 22 Sep. 2015. http://foreignpolicy.com/2015/05/15/china-liked-trans-pacific-partnership-until-u-s-officials-opened-their-mouths-trade-agreement-rhetoric-fail/.

BEATRIX BALOGH

US Citizenship of Overseas Territories

To denote a peculiar form of US Citizenship granted to Americans born and living in one of the US Overseas Territories I shall use the term *Insular Citizenship*. Neither regular, nor political or academic discourse make a uniform distinction in this matter.[1] Existing literature acknowledging the incongruities uneasily refers to it as incomplete, unequal, quasi, or second-class citizenship. After a brief overview of the main features of Insular Citizenship and the milestones of its acquisition, the paper will focus on recent trends and events that can potentially transform the citizenship debate from an academic question to an agenda-setting issue. The paper will identify research areas that are affected by the recent application of the infamous Insular Cases, and will also highlight how a US veteran's complaints about not being able to vote for President may gain attention in the upcoming presidential elections.

With the exception of American Samoa, large Insular Area possessions with indigenous local population are Organized Unincorporated Territories. In practical terms, the label denotes islands that have received local governments largely following the pattern of the US Constitution but are not incorporated into the Union, that is, are not States. Even though the term 'incorporated' remained undefined and gave rise to dissenting court opinions, 'incorporated territory' is most often described as one that

---

[1] No distinction is made in regular discourse.

Congress intends to make a state at some point in the future (Morrison 2013: 120). The status of these territories originates from the tension between the US Constitution and overseas expansion.

Although the Spanish American War of 1898 added Puerto Rico and Guam of the current territories to the United States, it was neither the beginning nor the end of overseas expansion. Though attempts at gaining foothold in the Caribbean in the 1860s failed (US Dept. of State), the concept of Insular Area territory was born a decade earlier with the passing of the Guano Islands Act in 1856. Not only did this law enable the annexation of small islands with guano deposits, some one hundred island territories over time (O'Donnell 44), it also changed the notion of new "territory" (Burnett 782). The concept was previously reserved for tracts of land that would in due course become an integral part of the United States, and as per the criteria outlined in the Northwest Ordinance of 1787, eventually a state. Commercial utility notwithstanding, the acquisitions of the Guano Islands established the precedent for eternal territorial status. But it was not until forty-five years later that the status question gained Constitutional relevance when the first Insular Cases challenging Puerto Rico's status reached the Supreme Court. American Samoa was annexed in 1900, the Virgin Islands in 1917, and the Northern Mariana Islands in 1947.

Unlike the uninhabited Guano Islands, the newly annexed territories were hoping to receive the full blessings of the US Constitution. However, citizenship did not follow the flag. Puerto Ricans lived in a "citizenship limbo," not being Spanish citizens already (although legally their citizenship was not revoked upon ceding the island to the United States), while the term "Puerto Rican citizen" did not mean much, since the island was not an independent country. Following President Roosevelt's promise in 1906 (1), and the ardent campaigning of Luis Muñoz Rivera, the Jones Act of Puerto Rico granted the islanders US citizenship in 1917 one month prior to US entry to World War I. In all subsequent cases (Virgin Islands in 1927, Guam in 1950, the Commonwealth of the Northern Mariana Islands in 1986) citizenship was granted by an Act of Congress, and not by the extension of the Constitution. American Samoans have remained US Nationals.

The territorial, non-state status is the primary source of the paradoxes inherent in Insular Citizenship. It is territorially determined, unstable, non-permanent, incomplete, and does not enjoy all constitutional guarantees. Residents of the islands cannot vote in the US federal elections because the US Constitution reserves that right for residents of States (Article 1, 2). Islanders cannot vote for President and enjoy only symbolic representation carried out by a Resident Commissioner for each island with voting rights in committees but not on the floor. Voting rights also change with residence. As US citizens, islanders can freely move to any of the fifty states where they enjoy full voting rights. The geographical proximity and long history of citizenship has brought about a divided Puerto Rican nation with 4 million possessing full voting rights, while another 4 million still partially disenfranchised. Transiency and insecurity stem from the statutory nature, and the various interpretations of the Fourteenth Amendment.[2] Since citizenship was accorded by an act of Congress, it can also be revoked by another act of Congress.[3] Thus, no constitutional rights to retain citizenship are guaranteed. Whereas in the past islanders voiced their concerns about the insecurities of their citizenship, incomplete franchise has lately received increased attention. Rather than seeking full voting rights by ordinary statute, as do the residents of the District of Columbia, also disenfranchised for lacking statehood (Coleman Tió 1389), islanders have seen the solution in elevating the political status. Even though statehood remains unattainable, one aspect of the citizenship paradox became both the elevator test and a potential agenda setter.

Many aspects of the democratic deficit remain hard to pin down for both insular and mainland Americans at large. The one question that sufficiently grasps the controversies and the one most Americans can easily identify with is *How come American Citizens of the United States Territories*

---

[2] It will later be expounded how the terminology interpretations of "born or naturalized in the jurisdiction thereof" excluded populations of Overseas Territories from the plenary guarantees of the Fourteenth Amendment.

[3] The possibility of revoking US citizenship was reasserted by Presidential Task Force Reports. Only the latest of these reports, published in 2011 with recommendations towards a status referendum, included a clause on retention of citizenship by those who possess US citizenship at the time irrespective of the referendum's results (*Report* 12).

who serve in large numbers in the United States Military and sacrifice their lives for a variety of US interests have no say in choosing their Commander-in Chief? Puerto Rico, Guam, and American Samoa are overrepresented in the US military (Kane, "Who Bears The Burden"). Reasons for enlisting are not merely pecuniary. Deputy Assistant Secretary for the Interior of Insular Affairs once noted that "[t]here is a very strong sense of patriotism throughout the US territories" adding that even a sitting Northern Marianas Congressman served a year in Iraq, whose reasons for doing it were clearly not economic (Teaiwa 325).

American military personnel with permanent residence in one of the fifty states can vote for the President by absentee ballot (Vergun 1). However, if permanent residence is in one of the Overseas Territories, the ballot would list candidates for local offices, but not for United States President (FVAP). The one exception to the rule is being stationed in one of the fifty states (Troy 1). If deployed overseas, in Iraq, Afghanistan, or any other hot spot, or their home island, for instance, the right to vote for President is not extended.

INSULAR CASES AND CURRENT APPLICATION

Although their US citizenship was acquired at various stages, legal rationale for denying citizenship rights is grounded in a series of law suits filed by corporations in the early years of the 20th century. The Insular Cases of 1901 refer to a series of Supreme Court decisions and opinions that are still applied in litigation involving status or citizenship.[4] In essence, the Court ruled that the constitution would not automatically follow the flag and officially introduced the concept of *territorial nonincorporation* (Gutierez 133). In practical terms, not only did the Insular Cases relegate the islands to eternal territorial status, but they also transformed the ideals of citizenship. Most scholars agree that the opinions reflected contemporary politics and attitude (Torruella 284-285). The irony of still being on the

---

[4] Legal scholars would extend the term to several later Supreme Court Cases, some as late as 1922, pertaining to the status of overseas territories (Torruella 284).

books has been repeatedly noted, and received reinvigorated attention in 2013 following up on *Tuaua* v. *United States*. Four American Samoans, US nationals born on US territory were denied citizenship rights in a D.C. District Court based on the 1901 ruling in *Downes* v. *Bidwell*. Perhaps the most infamous of the nine Insular Cases, the court ruled that citizenship can be denied to residents of overseas territories because they are "foreign to [...] the habits, traditions, and modes of life". Civil rights attorney Neil Weare argued the case in the Court of Appeals in January 2015 (US Court of Appeals). At issue was *what is, and what is not* "in the United States" (5). "Even if 'United States' is broader than 'among the several States,'" argued the court, "it remains ambiguous whether territories situated like American Samoa are 'within' the United States for purposes of the [citizenship] clause" (7). Following the July 2015 District Court opinion the case was subsequently filed for rehearing *en banc*. While the court applied the Insular Cases the petitioners argue that the Fourteenth Amendment is self-explicatory and its guarantees should be extended to all persons born in the United States.

THE CITIZENSHIP DEBATE MAKES WAVES

The case was widely reported in both the national media, and, not surprisingly, in local island media outlets. There has not been any practical change in the legal framework, but the direct and indirect impact of *Tuaua* is felt in several areas of political discourse, both theory and practice. Historical scholarship has principally focused on the causes and emergence of the American Empire. However, non-incorporation has lately received more attention in academic circles slowly shifting the focus of the debate.

Reconsidering The Insular Cases: the past and future of the American Empire, which originated from a Harvard Law School conference, takes a new critical view of the decisions and opinions that, suggest the authors, are "tinged with outdated notions of race and empire" and "have created a range of dilemmas for our age" (fourth cover). Most case studies in the book are based on the Puerto Rican experience, but Rogers Smith's paper on "Differentiated Citizenship" provides a solid background for a reinvigorated citizenship debate. Although Smith's study is still in the abstract, it takes into account challenges of Overseas Territories to existing models and recognizes the importance of "creating more meaningful equality of status" that can accommodate "distinct histories, aspirations and needs" (108). He also provides an overview of the history and controversies of what I call Insular Citizenship; the importance of which lies not in novelty of facts but the novelty of the issue being raised and discussed by a renowned American citizenship scholar. Hereto it has been a recurring subject of treatises written from the perspectives of local grievances, and occasionally taken up by scholars and experts dwelling in the legal intricacies – but remained a relatively arcane question.

Legal and sociological discourse on citizenship models in the United States recognizes two major challenges to US citizenship: immigration and globalization. The immigration laws of the United States divide the global population into two categories: US nationals and aliens (Gutierez 131). The extent and process of conferring rights to immigrants is widely debated. Forms and manifestations of transnationalism are now academic currency. However, citizenship models have not yet addressed the peculiar form of US citizenship held by Americans who are overseas as a result of moving "national" borders encompassing territories without the prospect of statehood. While the Insular Cases are both reasserted and challenged in court, the very model of US citizenship remains uncontested. Neither "foreign in a domestic sense" (Morrison 1), nor the "alien other" are accommodated by models applicable in the US.

Although Linda Kerber hesitantly arrived at the conclusion that in the aftermath of the Spanish American war, "the nation experimented with the creation of ambiguous spaces, between the domestic and the foreign," which, she adds later, "lay great potential for statelessness," this particular limbo status is typically discussed in the context of refugees (13, 20). In Peter H. Schruck's review none of the three possible models of citizenship, *Nationalistic*, *Human Rights* or *Marshallian* accommodates the form granted to overseas territories. He only makes a passing comment on how "[t]he incomplete American citizenship of Puerto Ricans and residents of the District of Columbia may illustrate [the] inhibitions" of limited voting rights in the United States in contrast to certain European practices that apply the human rights model (164). Also instructive is Roger Smith's earlier review of three books on American citizenship. In way of introduction, he reasserts the observable trends in US Citizenship Scholarship trying to accommodate immigrants with various statuses, and overseas Americans with multiple allegiances. He proposes that central to solving the conundrum is changing two ways of how Americans tend to think of citizenship: that it is a membership in a sovereign state and an essentially uniform status (907-908). For a variety of deviations from nation-state models membership of US Overseas Territories demonstrate these myths with vigor. Their status challenges many of the six norms for ideal-typical model of membership Roger Brubaker once outlined for benchmarking purposes (380-381). These anomalies are not rare in various countries with multiple nationalities, immigrant population, or denizens (Soysal 138-162). Yet, even if the norms originate from old notions of nation states, the apparent clash of the first two, *egalitarian*, and *sacred*, are incongruent with democratic-republican ideals. The first proposes that there should only be full membership and no other, "enduring gradation of membership". Persons awaiting naturalization is an obvious exception, but second-class citizenship is unacceptable, especially in light of the other membership norm that requires citizens to make sacrifices for the state, "prepared to die for it if need be" (Brubaker 380). It is perhaps the very reason why this second aspect of Insular Citizenship serves an effective elevator test and touches emotional chords – and can also become an agenda setting issue.

Undoubtedly not central to campaigns, but the upcoming primary season can see some vigorous verbal battles fought for equal rights, particularly in one constituency. Like other insular Americans, Puerto Ricans cannot vote in Presidential Elections, but they vote in the primaries. They also send superdelegates to national conventions. Yet, the most important impact of the Puerto Rican vote is felt in Florida. The 2012 status referendum, the previous primaries, the Floridan vote, and the debt crisis in the summer of 2014 all triggered increased attention to various aspects of Insular Citizenship. The continued exodus of Puerto Rican professionals to Florida, topped with the echo of *Tuaua* can further the islanders' quest for equality in the 2016 presidential elections. The emergence of the

Floridan Vote was acutely felt in the last presidential elections in 2012. Puerto Ricans settling in Florida dominate the Interstates 4 Corridor of Central Florida making the state more susceptible to their agenda. Carrying the one million Puerto Ricans of the I4 wins Florida and its 29 electors. With a growing political clout they can influence agenda. One intricate aspect of this voting bloc is that the vote they cast in Florida is also a vote on political status and equality, granting full-fledged democratic rights to Puerto Ricans.

Ira Rodriguez's migration palpably exemplifies the case. A San Juan native, she declared her preference for President in the Puerto Rico primaries in 2012, cheered for Obama as a superdelegate at the Democratic Convention but could cast no citizen vote in the Presidential elections upon returning to her home. The young attorney eventually moved to Florida to be able to exercise a fundamental right (Fox News). Jeffrey Rondon, a recent addition to the economic exodus from the island to Florida also acquired the vote by changing residence. He points out that his right to vote "is a privilege" that he wants to exercise (Jordan 1). Another transnational behavior pattern that should receive research attention is voting by proxy. Data on extent and potential is not yet analyzed but a marine veteran living in Puerto Rico suggested that he would "push all his siblings" and other relatives in Florida and New Jersey to vote. He also asked "[w]hy is it that I can't vote for the person who will send me to war?" (Fox News). Equality and citizenship rights were gaining center stage in political debates in 2012 and can potentially reframe the status discourse in the upcoming elections. It is a mandatory issue for candidates to address both in San Juan and Orlando.

Even though the territorial status of the islands is not likely to change in the near future, the democratic deficit inherent in Insular Citizenship has received increasing attention. Citizenship models have not yet accommodated the intricate membership of Insular Americans, who are neither immigrants nor overseas Americans by choice. On the other hand, ramifications of mounting awareness have reached courtrooms, and may stimulate historian scholarship on the nature of the Empire and can make waves in the upcoming elections.

References:

Brubaker, Roger. "Immigration, Citizenship, and the Nation-State in France and Germany: A Comparative Historical Analysis." *International Sociology* 5 (1990): 379-407. Print.

Burnett, Christina Duffy. "The Edges of Empire and the Limits of Sovereignty: American Guano Islands." *American Quarterly* 57.3 (2005): 779-803. Print.

Coleman Tió, José R. "Six Puerto Rican Congressmen go to Washington." *The Yale Law Journal* 116.6 (2007): 1389-1399. Print.

Downes v. Bidwell 182 US 244 (1901) *JUSTIA*. Web. 5 Jul. 2014. https://supreme.justia.com/cases/federal/us/182/244/case.html.

Fox News. "US-Based Puerto Ricans Want Equality, Right To Vote, Statehood Back Home." 1 Dec. 2013. Web. 15 Jan. 2014. http://latino.foxnews.com/latino/politics/2013/12/01/in-florida-puerto-ricans-want-equality-right-to-vote-statehood-back-home.

Federal Voting Assistance Program. Web. 20 May 2014. www.fvap.gov.

Gutierez, Hannah M. T. "Guam's Future Political Status: An Argument for Free Association with US Citizenship." *The Asian-Pacific Law and Policy Journal* 4.1 (2003): 122-149. Web. 3 May 2013. http://blog.hawaii.edu/aplpj/files/2011/11/APLPJ_04.1_gutierrez.pdf.

Jordan, Mary. "Exodus from Puerto Rico Could Upend the Florida Vote in 2016 Presidential Race." *The Washington Post* 26 Jul. 2015. Web. 26 Sep. 2015. http://www.washingtonpost.com/politics/exodus-from-puerto-rico-could-upend-florida-vote-in-2016-presidential-race/2015/07/26/d73bc724-3229-11e5-8353-1215475949f4_story.html.

Kane, Tim. "Who Bears the Burden? Demographic Characteristics of US Military Recruits Before and After 9/11." Center for Data Analysis Report #05-08 on National Security and Defense. *The Heritage Foundation*. 7 Nov. 2005. Web. 25 Aug. 2015. http://www.heritage.org/research/reports/2005/11/who-bears-the-burden-demographic-characteristics-of-us-military-recruits-before-and-after-9-11.

Kerber, Linda K. "Stateless as the Citizen's Other: A View from the United States." *The American Historical Review* 112.1 (2007): 1-34. Print.

Morrison, Sean. "Foreign in a Domestic Sense: American Samoa and the Last US Nationals." *Hastings Constitutional Law Quarterly* 41.1 (2013): 71-150. Print.

Neuman, Gerald E. and Tomiko Brown-Nagin. *Reconsidering The Insular Cases: the past and future of the American Empire.* Cambridge, MA: Harvard UP, 2015. Print.

O'Donnell, Dan. "The Pacific Guano Islands: The Stirring of the American Empire." *Pacific Studies* 16.1 (1993): 43-66. Print.

Report By the President's Task Force on Puerto Rico's Status. The White House. 11 Mar. 2011. Web. 5 May 2012. https://www.whitehouse.gov/sites/default/files/uploads/Puerto_Rico_Task_Force_Report.pdf.

Roosevelt, Theodore. "Message Regarding the State of Puerto Rico." 11 Dec. 1906. *Miller Center. Web.* 15 May 2015. http://millercenter.org/president/roosevelt/speeches/message-regarding-the-state-of-puerto-rico.

Schruck, Peter H. "Three Models of Citizenship." In: *Citizenship in America and Europe: Beyond the Nation State?* Eds. Michael S. Greeve and Michael Zöller. Washington D.C.: AEI, 2009: 151-184. Print.

Smith, Rogers M. "Beyond Sovereignty and Uniformity: The Challenges for Equal Citizenship in the Twenty-First Century." Book Review. *Harvard Law Review* 122.907 (2009): 907-937. Print.

—. "The Insular Cases, Differentiated Citizenship, and Territorial Statuses in the Twenty First Centrury." In: *Reconsidering The Insular Cases: The Past and Future of the American Empire.* Eds. Gerald E. Neuman and Tomiko Brown-Nagin. Cambridge, MA: Harvard UP, 2015. 104-128. Print.

Soysal, Yasemin. *Limits of Citizenship. Migrants and Postnational Membership in Europe.* Chicago: U of Chicago P, 1994. Print.

Teaiwa, Teresia K. "Globalizing and Gendered Forces: The Contemporary Militarization of Pacific/Oceania." In: *Gender and Globalization in Asia and the Pacific. Method, Practice, Theory.* Eds. Kathy E. Ferguson and Monique Mironesco. Honolulu: U of Hawaii P, 2008, 318-334. Print.

Torruella, Juan R. "The Insular Cases: the Establishment of a Regime of Political Apartheid." *U. Pa. J. Int'l L* 29.2 (2007): 283-347. Print.

Troy, Rolan A. "Re: RE: PhD student's question on voting rights of Puerto Ricans serving in the US military (UNCLASSIFIED)." 20 May 2014. Message to author. E-Mail.

United States. Court of Appeals, D.C. Circuit *Tuaua v United State*s. Web. 20 Sep. 2015. https://www.cadc.uscourts.gov/internet/opinions.nsf/A927D0D5D8A8FB0B85257E5B004F530D/$file/13-5272-1555940.pdf.

—. Dept. of State. Archive. "Purchase of the United States Virgin Islands, 1917." Web. 15 Aug. 2015 http://2001-2009.state.gov/r/pa/ho/time/wwi/107293.htm.

Vergun, David. "Soldiers Could Impact Direction of America – by Voting." *ARNEWS*. 11 Mar. 2014. Web. 20 May 2014. http://www.army.mil/article/121635/.

ANNA BARTNIK

Illegal, Undocumented or Unauthorized

A Few Reflections on Unauthorized Population in the United States

The United States of America is a country that has been one of the most desired destinations for immigrants since its creation. This popular belief has been proved by researchers many times. In 2010, Gallup (an American research-based company) published one of its migration findings. According to the numbers presented, 700 million adults worldwide would like to move to another country if they had such opportunity. Among them, there were more than 165 million who would choose the USA as their destination. Gallup's findings reveal only the desires of potential immigrants. Otherwise, if all these people had done as they wished, the US could have experienced a net population growth of 60% (Clifton). On the other hand, data show how deeply the myth of the American dream is rooted worldwide. This optimistic vision makes immigrants believe that once they cross the US border, they can live their American dream. Such popular belief causes a constant growth of the number of those who decide even to break US law and start their illegal stay in America.

After many years of huge immigrant inflow to the United States, in 2015, American researchers revealed that the number of unauthorized immigrants in the US has become stable. However, the new findings did not change the direction of public discourse on immigration in the US Immigration policy usually attracts the attention of public opinion when Americans feel under threat. Such a situation occurred after the 9/11 terrorist attacks in 2001, and the Tsarnaevs' bombing during the Boston

Marathon in 2013 or the most recent (at the time when this article was written) shootings in San Bernardino, California. Such tragedies lead to more questions on national security, which is inextricably connected with immigration, both legal and illegal.

In November 2014, the immigration issue again became a focal point of the political debate, when president Barack Obama announced his executive order. He proposed a program expanding deportation relief to an impressive number (about 5 million) of the unauthorized immigrant population living in the US (Office of the Press Secretary, the White House). Although President Obama's project is on hold[1], as a result of a court challenge brought about by several states (Hereskovitz), presidential action has been considered the most significant step in improving the situation of illegal immigrants since Reagan's amnesty in 1986. Moreover, the refugee crisis in Europe and Obama's plan to admit 85,000 foreign refugees in the fiscal year 2016 strengthened the debate on immigration, especially in the time of the forthcoming presidential elections.

The main purpose of this article is to show some issues connected with unauthorized immigrants' presence in the US and to present the basic, but also the most recent, trends in illegal immigration. The article also focuses on differences between words or phrases used to describe the unauthorized immigrant population.[2] It also discusses who crosses the border illegally, and how. The constant inflow of strangers has influenced every aspect of American life, but Americans are rather consistent in their opinion on immigration and immigrants. Their anti-immigrant feelings are affected most often by accidental tragedies and their anti-immigrant anger grows in the immediate aftermath of such events, but some time later their attitudes towards immigration go back to previous levels. Such a situation occurred after one of the biggest tragedies in American history, the World Trade Center terrorist attack in 2001. Shortly after the attack, Americans were more likely to say they had a negative opinion

---

[1] As of 16 Jan. 2016.

[2] It is easy to be misunderstood while using terms describing the population living in the USA without permission. This article does not intend to support or criticize any usage. As the dispute over labeling immigrants is not finished and there is no clear and convincing way of using neutral terms, I will use the term "unauthorized immigrant".

on immigrants. But after a few years, their attitude towards immigrants resembled that before the attacks (Suro).

Since the second part of the 20th century, the term "political correctness" has gained more attention in public discourse. It appeared that choosing the right word had become a very important issue. By using "politically incorrect" language one was put at a risk of being accused of xenophobia, racism, or other similarly offensive attitudes. Political correctness also changed the world of words and phrases used to describe those who were staying in the US illegally. Since then, the term "illegal immigrant" became a wrong one, implying a negative attitude toward a huge group of people and considered to be incorrect as only an action can be "illegal", not a person. Such point of view was favored by pro-immigrant organizations. They shared the idea with social media like Facebook, Twitter, YouTube, etc., but also asked traditional media not to refer to people as "illegal" in their articles and videos. This campaign was named "Drop the I-Word" and was launched in 2010. It resulted in a partial success. The Center for Racial Justice Innovation and the Applied Research Center, responsible for the campaign, concluded: "although the Associated Press, USA Today, LA Times, and many other news outlets and journalist associations have dropped the i-word, this racial slur in still being used in the media and everyday language" (www. raceforward.org). The idea was widely discussed, as many immigration supporters did not agree with it. Mark Krikorian, the executive director of the Center for Immigration Studies, agreed that the term "illegal immigrant" was not accurate. In his opinion, it was not precise to refer to a foreigner staying unlawfully in the US as an "illegal immigrant", although it was still acceptable in common usage. The definition of the term "immigrant", in American law, says that an immigrant is a person who has been granted lawful permanent residence (Leitsinger 2012). Discussing Krikorian's explanation, it is necessary to look more carefully into American law. The Department of Homeland Security (DHS) revealed the official position on the definition problems and stated as follows:

> Permanent Resident Alien – An alien admitted to the United States as a lawful permanent resident. Permanent residents are also commonly referred to as immigrants; however, the Immigration and Nationality Act

(INA) broadly defines an immigrant as any alien in the United States, except one legally admitted under specific nonimmigrant categories (INA section 101(a)(15)). An illegal alien who entered the United States without inspection, for example, would be strictly defined as an immigrant under the INA but is not a permanent resident alien. Lawful permanent residents are legally accorded the privilege of residing permanently in the United States. They may be issued immigrant visas by the Department of State overseas or adjusted to permanent resident status by the Department of Homeland Security in the United States. (www.dhs.gov)

Kevin R. Johnson, the dean of the UC Davis School of Law, emphasizes that such commonly used terms as "illegal immigrant" or "illegal alien" can be found nowhere in American federal law. Moreover, they equate an unauthorized immigrant with a criminal, while the person in question may not have committed any crime at all. It also implies that such individual should be punished. He suggests using more neutral terms as "an undocumented alien". Johnson's and many other researchers' point of view is not shared by the media (Davis 50). Journalists from the Associated Press declared using more euphemistic terms such as "living in the country without legal permission". They argued that a different meaning was implied while using the word "undocumented". This term suggested that the problem was minor, connected with missing a proper document and needing only simple paperwork to be done. Meanwhile, the situation of "undocumented" people was far more serious. Their everyday life was influenced by the threat of being arrested and deported (Leitsinger 2012). Others also noted that the term "undocumented immigrants" may be misleading as it suggested they had no documents. Aliens residing in the US, even without authorization, possessed documents such as passports, US driver's licenses, school IDs, etc. (Golash-Boz). For this reason, the Migration Policy Institute[3] decided to use the term "unauthorized migrant" as the most neutral and complete when referring to people staying in foreign countries without permission. It also did not criminalize immigrants (Van Hook).

---

[3] The Migration Policy Institute (MPI) is an independent, non-partisan, non-profit think tank dedicated to the study of the movement of people worldwide.

Hispanics, as the most numerous minority group in the US, have also engaged in the Drop the I-word campaign (Arreola 18). Their share in American society is significant and visible enough to make them an important actor on the American political scene, especially, when in the question of illegal/unauthorized population in the US. According to the DHS' Office of Immigration Statistics in 2014, there were over 11 million undocumented immigrants living in the US. Most of them were of Hispanic origin (Zong and Batalova). When the New York Times refused to join the Drop the I-Word campaign and continued to use the term "illegal immigrant", Univision, an American Spanish language broadcast television network, criticized the decision.[4] Latino activists, in a series of statements, condemned the New York Time's attitude and proved that the newspaper used to allow offensive terms in its pages in the past. Among them, there was the term "wetbacks", considered to be particularly discriminating for Mexican immigrants (Planas). It referred to illegal border crossers who decided to swim across the Rio Grande river. During the debate a surprising fact was revealed. Cesar Chavez, the well-known Latino activist and co-founder of the United Farm Workers union, also used the terms "wetbacks" and "illegals" to describe undocumented workers hired to break strikes.[5] This was proved by an interview recorded in September 25, 1972, in which Cesar Chavez shared his views on American border problems using these controversial words (Lord).

The official language of the American government prefers using the terms "illegal alien" or "illegal immigrant". Sometimes these names become more specific, e.g. "criminal alien" or "fugitive alien", but all of them are also considered by human rights supporters as not accurate, dehumanizing and discriminating.

Looking closer into the debate on labeling aliens, it is clear that Americans have encountered difficulties in their choice of language as a result of political correctness. Although there are many different terms in use,

---

[4] Although the New York Times was not the only representative media to state that it was still going to use that term, it was considered a leader in the American media market, and one that set the tone for others.

[5] More on Cesar Chavez and the United Farm Workers Union in: Bartnik 7-21.

it appears that none of them is accurate. These terms have also become a part of the political game. The term "undocumented immigrant" is often used by immigration supporters. Anti-immigrant groups tend to use the term "illegal immigrant", as it stresses the fact of violation of the existing law. Summarizing arguments against using the term "illegal immigrant", it is clear that objections are based on two grounds: legal and moral. The legal grounds include (Batra Kashyap) the following:

- the term is legally misleading because it connotes criminality, while presence in the US without proper documents is a civil offense, not a criminal one;
- it is legally inaccurate because it is akin to calling a criminal defendant "guilty" before a verdict is rendered;
- it is legally imprecise because it implies finality even though immigration status is fluid and, depending on individual circumstances, can be adjusted;
- it is technically inaccurate because it labels the individual as opposed to the actions the person has taken.

The moral grounds include the following reasons:
- the term scapegoats individual immigrants for problems that are largely systemic;
- the term divides and dehumanizes communities and is used to discriminate against people of color;
- the term creates an environment of hate by exploiting racial fear;
- the term affects attitudes toward immigrants and non-immigrants alike, most often toward people of African, Asian, Central American and Mexican descent;
- the term impacts the way young people feel about themselves and their place in the world;
- the term increases the tolerance of the American public for daily violations of human rights;
- the term is a code word for racial and ethnic hatred;
- the term is outdated, offensive, and implicitly carries with it negative connotations.

The most popular explanation of the term "unauthorized immigrant" states that this term refers to a person who resides in the US illegally, but such a definition is not complete. There are, at least, two basic types of "unauthorized immigrants" (Hoefer, Rytina and Baker). First, immigrants who crossed the border without inspection. There are many different ways of entering American territory illegally. Every day and night individuals, as well as organized groups, are trying to clandestinely enter the US, most often at the southern border. Despite all efforts taken by the American administration, immigrants still manage to avoid many of the security measures implemented on the Mexican-American border. The wall built at the border, reinforced by specialized high-tech equipment, does not stop immigrants from crossing. The Border Patrol reports about smugglers tunnels under the fence, catapults used to smuggle drugs, the use of gas blowpipes to cut the fence. Some tunnels are impressive. In 2015, CNN informed about the most recent "super tunnel" found by border agents. The tunnel extended over the length of eight football fields, and had a rail system, lighting, electricity and metal beams to prevent collapse. It was the tenth large-scale smuggling tunnel discovered in the San Diego area alone since 2006. In all, more than 75 cross-border smuggling tunnels were discovered, mostly in California and Arizona (Martinez).

Building a fence along the Mexican-American border is still a controversial issue. It costs a huge amount of money and provides an imperfect security. The issue was raised by Donald Trump, one of the 2016 presidential candidates, who favored the idea of the fence as a barrier that would stop the inflow of foreigners entering the United States illegally (Drew). Thad Bingel, a former senior US Customs and Border Protection official who was involved in border fence-building during the George W. Bush administration, commented on Trump's propositions: "Every wall can be circumvented. People can go under it, they can go over it. … No one should go into this with the idea that if you just build the right kind of wall, no one will get through" (Markon).

The second meaning of the term "unauthorized immigrant" refers to the so called "visa overstayers". These are foreigners who entered the United States with a valid visa, but stayed after its expiration date. Once they stayed longer than they were allowed, they became unauthorized.

The group represents an estimated 40% of the 11 million unauthorized immigrants living in the USA. In 2016, the Department of Homeland Security released its first ever report on "visa overstayers", a population that was largely unknown (Entry/Exit Overstay Report. Fiscal Year 2015). Previous attempts of counting and describing these immigrants had failed. The data released by the DHS indicate that those who overstayed their visas were only a small part of all foreigners who entered the US legally. Respectively, 482 781 and nearly 45 million in fiscal year 2015 (Gomez). Additional studies described this group in detail. "Visa overstayers" were better educated than those who crossed the border without authorization. They also spoke better English. The findings of the Californian Public Policy Institute revealed that about 55% of them speak English well or very well compared with 39% of those who crossed the border illegally (Murray).

In 2014, there were 11.3 million unauthorized immigrants living in the US. From 2009 to 2014 the number remained rather stable. Since the 1990s, the population of those staying in the US illegally had been continuously rising. In 1990, they numbered 3.5 million and the number peaked in 2007 to 12.2 million. At that point, there was a sudden decrease, generated mostly by diminishing Mexican immigration to the US. In 2012, an estimated 6 million unauthorized Mexican immigrants were residing in America, representing more than half of the total unauthorized population in the US (Bruno). Since 2009, there have been about 100 000 new Mexicans annually entering the country without authorization. However, when the recession began the northern neighbor became less popular as an immigration destination. In 2014, 5.6 million unauthorized immigrants from Mexico resided in the USA, representing 49% of the total unauthorized population (Gonzalez-Barrera and Krogstad).

Analyzing more data on unauthorized immigrants in the United States, it is evident that they replicate migration patterns known from the general characteristics of immigration processes in the US. California, New York, New Jersey, Florida and Nevada are considered the so-called "immigration states" – they have the largest immigrant population in their territory (Krogstad and Keegan). These states are also among the most popular destinations for unauthorized immigrants (Bruno).

Unauthorized immigrants are mostly attracted by work opportunities offered by the American economy. New trends appeared in 2007 that affected immigrant workforce. Data revealed by the Pew Research Center shows that the unauthorized immigrant workforce hold fewer blue-collar jobs and more white-collar ones. Surprisingly, the changing economy did not influence the distribution of unauthorized laborers among different occupational groups. They occupied low skilled service positions (33%), construction and extraction (15%), production, installation and repair (14%) (Passel and Cohn). Overall data differed among states. For example, in southern states the construction industry employed more unauthorized immigrant workers than any other, while manufacturing dominated mostly in the Midwest.

Unauthorized immigrants made up a larger share of the labor force than of the overall population, the Pew Research Center data said. The reason was immigrants' age. The unauthorized population is predominantly a young population, particularly of working age. Most of the population lived with their families; almost half of them were couples with children. In 2008 73% of unauthorized immigrant parents' children were American citizens by birth. The number of children born in the US in mixed-status families (families where one parent is an unauthorized immigrant while the other is an American citizen) has been rising since 2003. Meanwhile, the number of children born in the USA to two unauthorized parents has hardly changed (Passel and Cohn).

In 2015 the Center for Migration Studies released a report stating that the number of unauthorized immigrants in the USA had fallen below 11 million. It is impossible to name one specific reason responsible for this decline. This was rather the effect of many combined reasons. The first of these was a tighter border control. Using modern technology, building the fence and increasing the number of border patrol agents resulted in more effective apprehensions at the border. The situation was also influenced by economic and demographic changes that occurred in Mexico. The data also revealed that the characteristic of a typical immigrant changed. Previously, in most cases it was a young man. Then, according to the data, it was a person who was 35 or older and had lived in the USA for a decade or more (Markon b). Researchers also noticed that restrictive state immigration laws were not as effective as expected. Despite the new trends and reasons one thing has not changed so far – hundreds of thousands of new unauthorized immigrants continue to settle in the United States every year.

REFERENCES:

Arreola, Daniel. *Hispanic Spaces, Latino Places: Community and Cultural Diversity in Contemporary America*. Austin: University of Texas Press, 2009. Print.

Bartnik, Anna. "Awakening the Sleeping Giant – a Short History of Hispanics Organizations in California and Texas." *Ad Americam* 7 (2006). Print.

Batra Kashyap, Monika. *"Illegal" vs. "Undocumented": A NWIRP Board Member's Perspective*. Web. 5 Feb. 2016 https://www.nwirp.org/illegal-vs-undocumented-a-nwirp-board-members-perspective/.

Bruno, Andorra. "Unauthorized Aliens in the United States." Congressional Research Service. 8 May 2014. Web. 8 Feb. 2016. https://fas.org/sgp/crs/homesec/R41207.pdf.

Clifton, Jon. *Roughly 6.2 Million Mexicans Express Desire to Move to US*. n.d. Web. 26 Jan. 2016 http://www.gallup.com/poll/139391/Roughly-Million-Mexicans-Express-Desire-Move.aspx.

Davis, John H. *United States of America -- Right Now*. Xlibris Corporation, 2014.

Department of Homeland Security. "Definition of Terms." n.d. Web. 30 Jan. 2016. http://www.dhs.gov/definition-terms#permanent_resident_alien.

Drew, Kate. "This Is what Trump's Border Wall Could Cost US." CNBC. 9 Oct. 2015. Web. 6 Feb. 2016. http://www.cnbc.com/2015/10/09/this-is-what-trumps-border-wall-could-cost-us.html.

"Entry/Exit Overstay Report. Fiscal Year 2015." 19 01 2016. US Department of Homeland Security. 19 Jan. 2016. Web. 7 Feb. 2016. https://www.dhs.gov/sites/default/files/publications/FY%2015%20DHS%20Entry%20and%20Exit%20Overstay%20Report.pdf.

Golash-Boza, Tanya. "No Human Being is Illegal: It's Time to Drop the 'I-word'." *Aljazzera*. 8 Apr. 2013. Web. 5 Feb. 2016. http://www.aljazeera.com/indepth/opinion/2013/04/201347111531424247.html.

Gomez, Alan. "Nearly 500K Foreigners Overstayed Visas in 2015." *USA Today* 20 Jan. 2016. Web. 6 Feb. 2016. http://www.usatoday.com/story/

news/2016/01/19/immigration-visa-overstays-department-of-homeland-security-report/79026708/.

Gonzalez-Barrera, Ana and Jens Manuel Krogstad. "What We Know about Illegal Immigration from Mexico." Pew Research Center. 20 Nov. 2015. Web. 8 Feb. 2016. http://www.pewresearch.org/fact-tank/2015/11/20/what-we-know-about-illegal-immigration-from-mexico/.

Hereskovitz, Jon. Reuters. 3 Dec. 2014. Web. 16 Jan. 2016. http://www.reuters.com/article/us-usa-immigration-lawsuit-idUSKCN0JH2EI20141203.

Hoefer, Michael, Rytina, Nancy and Bryan Baker. "Estimates of the Unauthorized Immigrant Population Residing in the United States: January 2011." Department of Homeland Security. March 2012. Web. 10 Feb. 2016. http://www.dhs.gov/sites/default/files/publications/ois_ill_pe_2011_0.pdf.

Krogstad, Jens Manuel and Michael Keegan. "15 States with the Highest Share of Immigrants in Their Population." Pew Research Center. 14 May 2014. Web. 8 Feb. 2016. http://www.pewresearch.org/fact-tank/2014/05/14/15-states-with-the-highest-share-of-immigrants-in-their-population/.

Leitsinger, Miranda S. "Drop the 'I' Word? Debating the Term "Illegal Immigrant"." *NBC News*. 11 Jul. 2012. Web. 30 Jan. 2016. http://usnews.nbcnews.com/_news/2012/07/11/12664426-drop-the-i-word-debating-the-term-illegal-immigrant?lite.

Lord, Jeffrey. "Cesar Chavez: Anti-Immigration to His Union Core." *The American Spectator* 15 Jul. 2014. Web. 1 Feb. 2016. http://spectator.org/articles/59956/cesar-chavez-anti-immigration-his-union-core.

Markon, Jerry. "Trump Says Building a US-Mexico Wall is 'Easy.' But Is it Really?" *The Washington Post* 17 Jul. 2015. Web. 6 Feb. 2016. https://www.washingtonpost.com/politics/trump-on-the-us-mexico-border-building-a-wall-is-easy/2015/07/16/9a619668-2b0c-11e5-bd33-395c05608059_story.html.

—. "US Illegal Immigrant Population Falls Below 11 million, Continuing Nearly Decade-Long Decline, Report Says." *The Washington Post* 20 Jan. 2016. Web. 11 Feb. 2016. https://www.washingtonpost.com/news/federal-eye/wp/2016/01/20/u-s-illegal-immigrant-population-falls-below-11-million-continuing-nearly-decade-long-decline-report-says/.

Martinez, Michael. "Feds Raid Drug 'Super Tunnel' with Railway on US-Mexico Border." CNN. 24 Oct. 2015. Web. 6 Feb. 2016. http://edition.cnn.com/2015/10/23/us/drug-super-tunnel-tijuana-san-diego/.

Murray, Sara. "Many in US Illegally Overstayed Their Visas." *The Wall Street Journal* 7 Apr. 2013. Web. 7 Feb. 2016. 07 02 2016. http://www.wsj.com/articles/SB10001424127887323916304578404960101110032.

Office of the Press Secretary, the White House. *Immigration Accountability Executive Action*. 20 Nov. 2014. Web. 16 Jan. 2016. https://www.whitehouse. gov/the-press-office/2014/11/20/fact-sheet-immigration-accountability-executive-action.

Passel Jeffrey S. and Cohn D'Vera. "A Portrait of Unauthorized Immigrants in the United States." The Pew Research Center. 14 Apr. 2009. Web. 10 Feb. 2016. http://www.pewhispanic.org/2009/04/14/a-portrait-of-unauthorized-immigrants-in-the-united-states/.

—. "Share of Unauthorized Immigrant Workers in Production, Construction Jobs Falls Since 2007." The Pew Research Center. 26 Mar. 2015. Web. 10 Feb. 2016. http://www.pewhispanic.org/2015/03/26/share-of-unauthorized-immigrant-workers-in-production-construction-jobs-falls-since-2007/.

Planas, Roque. "'Illegal Immigrant' Debate: Univision Takes On The New York Times." *The Huffington Post* 8 Oct. 2012. Web. 1 Feb. 2016. http://www. huffingtonpost.com/2012/10/08/illegal-immigrant-debate-_n_1948904. html.

Suro, Roberto. "America's Views of Immigration: The Evidence From Public Opinion Surveys." 2009. The Migration Policy Institute. 2009. Web. 16 Jan. 2016. www.migrationpolicy.org/pubs/TCM-USPublicOpinion.pdf.

The Center for Racial Justice Innovation. *Race Forward*. n.d. Web. 30 Jan. 2016. https://www.raceforward.org/practice/tools/drop-i-word-campaign.

Van Hook, Jennifer, Bean, Frank D. and Jeffrey Passel. "Unauthorized Migrants Living in the United States: A Mid-Decade Portrait." *The Online Journal of the Migration Policy Institute* 1 Sep. 2005. Web. 5 Feb. 2016. http://www.migrationpolicy.org/article/unauthorized-migrants-living-united -states-mid-decade-portrait/.

Zong, Jie and Jeanne Batalova. "Frequently Requested Statistics on Immigrants and Immigration in the United States." Migration Policy Institute. 26 Feb. 2015. Web. 1 Feb. 2016. http://www.migrationpolicy.org/article/frequently-request-ed-statistics-immigrants-and-immigration-united-states#Unauthorized%20 Immigration.

EMŐKE HORVÁTH

The Departure of the Covadonga

The Catholic Clergy after the Triumph of the Cuban Revolution
(1960-1961)

In September of 1961, one hundred and thirty-one – old and young –
Catholic priests watched despondently from aboard the Spanish ship,
the *Covadonga*, as it left the Cuban shores to eventually reach its harbor
across the ocean. In my study, I will endeavor to reveal the factors that
compelled, or forced, these one hundred and thirty-one priests to leave
Cuba behind all at the same time.

After the victory of the Revolution on the 1st of January, 1959, the
Cuban Primate and the majority of the Catholic community in general,
enthusiastically welcomed the warriors who had overthrown the dicta-
torship of Fulgencio Batista. Enrique Pérez Serantes released his first
circular letter under the title of *Vida Nueva*[1] which greeted Fidel Castro
and the Revolution with hopeful anticipation. Castro's sense of mission
received intensive support from Catholic authorities and the standard
members of both the congregation and church leadership; not only did
it gain complete acceptance, but legitimacy and charisma as well through
certain regulations. The country's most influential Catholic newspaper,
the *Diario de la Marina*, presented Castro as a delegate of Providence; the
La Quincena in turn characterized him as a Jesus-like figure along with

---

[1] For an analysis of the circular, see: Horváth.

Camilo Cienfuegos, another emblematic personality of the Revolution.[2] This messianic vision had permeated even the level of the average person, a fact best proven by the remark of a Cuban housewife, according to whom "Fidel Castro represents Christ's thoughts" (Fernández 74). The powerful Catholic support was fed by the Church's view that "the directives of the Revolution ...are based on fundamental Christian principles" (Boza Masdival 615-616). After the fall of Batista's corrupt, dictatorial governance, society had high moral expectations for the representatives of the new system, which Castro further incited by emphasizing the image of the ascetic revolutionary. A significant part of Cuban society – including members of the white Catholic middle-class – eagerly awaited the country's political and economic rebirth, its democratization and the call for elections.

In 1960 the Catholic Church was concerned with the Soviet expansion in Cuba, a concern further intensified on May 8th when Cuba established diplomatic relations with the Soviet Union. Khrushchev's announcement in July that the Soviet Union would employ any means necessary to prevent the USA's armed intervention against Cuba and the signing of the first military agreement meant an even higher commitment on both sides.[3]

It is highly likely that these events have directly inspired Pérez Serantes to write the circular letter, *Por Dios y por Cuba*, in which he defines the connection between Catholic believers and Communism based on Pope Pius XI's *Divini Redemptoris* encyclical, and in this sense, judges Communism to be inherently evil. He states that Communism is based on Marx's dialectical materialism; it is only susceptible to material reality and claims to be atheist. With matter as its perpetual starting point, it denies all human values. In Communism, the people suffer from lack of freedom and moral breaks; they deny the marital bond and the right of ownership. Catholics are to have only one possible attitude towards Communism: follow the teachings of the Pope. The circular makes a strong distinction between the ideology (communism) and its representatives (communists); according to it, in the case of the latter the believer has

---

[2] *Diario de la Marina* 9 Jan. 1959. Print; *La Quincena* 6 Mar. 1959: 1A. Print.

[3] *Revolución* 21 Jul. 1960: 1. Print.

the right to exercise the Divine commandment of love (Pérez Serantes 55-59). My opinion is that, compared to the tone of the Primate's earlier writings, this circular is unusually harsh and firm, implacably rejective of the Communist ideology. His intended fight against it involves the spreading of Catholicism, the strengthening of religious education, and evangelization, the overcoming of religious ignorance.

Pérez Serantes' circular was read aloud in churches, but according to Ignacio Uría, it became quite widely known, so far so that the Primate even achieved international impact through it; James O. Eastland Democratic senator had asked the CIA's director for an English translation of the letter (Uría 378-379). The authorities' response was published in the pro-government newspaper *Sierra Maestra*; they issued an attack on Pérez Serantes for not unveiling the true enemy, North-American imperialism. The Primate was vehemently criticized on radio and in the columns of the *Hoy* as well (Uría 2011: 379).

The next huge political echo-triggering event was the joint circular of the Cuban Bishops (*Circular Colectiva del Episcopado Cubano*), issued on the 7th of August, 1960 (Circular Colectiva del Episcopado Cubano 60-62). The writing was virtually a reiteration of the Primate's concerns on behalf of the entire senior Catholic clergy. They recognized the resulting positive social changes of the Revolution, but they believed that they must maintain the same openness in voicing their concerns. They established that in recent times Cuba had developed intensive trade, cultural and diplomatic ties with the Soviet Union and several of the other socialist countries. Both journalists and high-ranking state officials have commended the systems of these countries, emphasizing the features that were in common with or similar to the Cuban Revolution. The Episcopate is highly troubled by this issue – the circular states – because Catholicism and Communism are completely opposite concepts. The letter goes on to explain the condemnation of Communism. They reject it because it is atheistic, it takes action against the clergy and it denies basic human rights.

The circular contained practically no new elements compared to the Primate's document, its importance lay more in the fact that it was signed by both Archbishops and all diocesan bishops; therefore it can be considered the uniform opinion, the common stance of the Catholic leadership and the ratification of Pérez Serantes' statement at the same time. The writing sparked anger of the authorities even though the *Diario de la Marina* – where the high-profile ecclesiastical circulars have previously been published – could no longer print it due to the newspaper's closing on the 12th of May. The radical cut-back on TV programs and the absence of the press also meant that the only influence that could be counted on was that of the circulars read out in churches, which, judging by the number of believers who attended Mass regularly, must have been very slight. However, the power saw to it that the masses were kept informed of the hostility of the Church leadership. The Meeting of Sugar Cane Cooperative Coordinators ended on the 10th of August, an event which offered an opportunity for Castro's public offensive against the Church.[4] The speaker dealt with the enemies of the Revolution throughout the entire duration of his speech mentioning, on the one hand, North-American imperialism, while on the other hand, the clergy who supported the fascist Franco. He permissively acknowledged that not all priests are fascists, but he noted that Franco may count on the support of such fascist priests in Cuba who incite their flock against the Revolution. He interpreted the contents of the circular for those in attendance as a condemnation of the Revolution. In this case, Fidel Castro had mercilessly taken advantage of the previously characterized incident when the Spanish-born monks had stood by Franco and, despite his remark, projected his resentment toward them practically onto the entire clergy, presenting them as Francoist Spaniards. He did this even though only two of the high priests were Spanish and neither of them had protested in favor of Franco.

The authorities sought to prevent the reading of the circular in churches and the State's anti-clerical attitude became generally more intense. Priests were arrested[5] and churches were attacked in their quest to make the Church an impossibility in every aspect. This was the starting point

---

[4] Discurso pronunciado por el Comandante Fidel Castro Ruz, primer ministro del gobierno revolucionario, en la clausura de la Rreunión de Coordinadores de Cooperativas Cañeras, en el Teatro de la CTC Revolucionaria, el 10 de agosto de 1960. Web. 2 Aug. 2015. http://www.cuba.cu/gobierno/discursos/1960/esp/f100860e.html.

[5] Priests Agnelio Blanco and Fernando Arango were arrested for reading out the circular and four members of the Acción Católica have also been questioned. See: Castro Figueroa.

of a nation-wide anti-religious campaign, another ecclesiastical document claims.[6] The State sought to cause turmoil within the ranks of the Catholic Church and supported the appearance and actions of "new Catholic" groups. Among them, the one that most vehemently opposed the official Church was the group that went by the name of *Con la Cruz y con la Patria*[7] (*With the Cross and the Homeland*). We know from Pérez Serantes' circular, entitled *Vivamos en paz* (*Let Us Live in Peace*), that in various Cuban cities such as Havana, Camagüey, Manzanillo, Bayamo and Santiago de Cuba, the "new Catholics" forcibly prevented clerical documents from being read out in churches and caused disruption during mass in a provocative manner (Pérez Serantes 79-82). The most serious incident occurred on the 13th of November, 1960 after the evening mass in the cathedral of Santiago de Cuba, when the conflicts between the priest who had performed the mass and the "new Catholics" had nearly degenerated into a fight; a week later, the same scene was repeated in Manzanillo. Based on the circular, it seems that the *Con la Cruz y con la Patria* might have been especially active in the Oriente province – the center of the fights against Batista – which in my opinion, in addition to the symbolic political significance of the region, can be explained by the fact that the Primate's residence was located in this southern region, a reality which in itself invited a more violent reaction and greater resistance from the new group.

From 1960 on, political resistance against Castro's government strived to adopt an increasingly more organized structure. According to the March 13th issue of *The New York Times* in 1960, there were five anti-Castro groups in existence in Miami.[8] The five groups were the *Movimiento Rescate Revolucionario* (Revolutionary Saviors' Movement), the *Movimiento Democrático Cristiano* (Christian Democratic Movement), *Movimiento de Recuperación Revolucionario* (Movement for the Restoration of the Revolution), the *Asociación Montecristi* (Montecristi Association) and the *Frente Nacional Democrático* (National Democratic Front), organizations which

---

[6] Carta abierta del episcopado al Dr. Fidel Castro Ruz. Web. 2 Aug. 2015.

[7] The group leaders were Antonio Pruna, Lula Horstman and Germán Lence (priest).

[8] *The New York Times* 13 Mar. 1960: 1. Print.

later joined forces under the name of *Frente Revolucionario Democrático* (Revolutionary Democratic Front). Catholics were also involved with the groups; in this respect, the *Movimiento Democrático Cristiano* which operated under the leadership of José Ignacio Rasco is particularly noteworthy. From a political point of view, the Cuban resistance presented a quite complex image. There were those among them who had been supporters of the Batista regime and had to flee the country after the Revolution, but the majority was made up of people who had participated in the anti-Batista fights and had supported Fidel Castro's goals immediately after the victory of the Revolution, but distanced themselves as communist ideas came to the forefront. José Miró Cardona, the first Prime Minister of the new Cuban power, Antonio Varona who also fulfilled the role of the country's Prime Minister between 1948 and 1950 and Manuel Ray, the new government's first Minister of Public Affairs, among others, can all be included in the latter group. Furthermore, Manuel Artime who was put in charge of the political leadership, had served as a lieutenant in Castro's insurrectionary army (*Cuba* 101).

After having broken off all diplomatic ties to Cuba on the 3rd of January 1961, a change occurred in the attitude of the US in March, when Dwight D. Eisenhower authorized a covert operation against Castro's regime, the fundamental aims of which included covering up the US's intention to intervene.[9] In May, the CIA launched the broadcast of *Radio Swan* to initiate a counter-propaganda – propaganda against the political power in Havana (Blasier 63).[10] The US tried to channel the emotions of Cuban emigrants and that of the anti-revolutionary forces remaining on the island and keep it flowing in a single bed by organizing the political and military resistance.[11] According to CIA estimates, in the spring of 1960, an approximately 2,500 to 3,000-strong team was readily available in Cuba to move against Castro's forces. In addition, as we see

---

[9] CIA document No. CIA 00027, 16 Mar. 1960. Web. 10 Aug. 2015.

[10] The name originated from the radio's location of its central office on the Swan Islands in the Carribbean Sea, off the coast of Hunduras.

[11] The evidence regarding the operation's organization can be found in the CIA's document labeled CIA 00027, 16 Mar. 1960. Web. 10 Aug. 2015.

it, about 25 percent of the population would have lent their support in the event of an attack, 20 percent would have expressed resistance while the remaining numbers would have declared neutrality.[12] In November of 1960, the CIA provided training for five hundred Cubans on a secret military base in Guatemala, however, news leaked out about the initiative (Rabe 166-176). That was probably the reason why Fidel Castro stated in his speech on the last day of the year that there are tens of thousands of armed Cubans in and around the capital to prevent any sudden external attacks on the country, "the insidious strike of imperialism."[13] Finally, on April 17th, 1961, the 1500-strong troop of the 2506 military unit made up of Cuban volunteers landed on the coast of the Bay of Pigs near the Zapata Peninsula with three priests serving as army chaplains as members of their escort.[14] The endeavor ended in a huge fiasco for the US, whereas the operation proved to be a success for Castro, who had personally led the defense and once again emerged politically stronger from the fight. The offensive was successfully repelled in less than two days and 1,180 people had been taken captive whose interrogation and trial took place publicly on television with Fidel Castro's active participation (*Cuba* 102).

Castro's speech at the 1st of May festivities in 1961 had obviously dealt at length with the events of the previous few days. He claimed that all three priests involved in the invasion were Spanish, moreover, to his knowledge they were Falangist priests and they had not arrived simply to serve the Church. However, a written appeal was found in the notebook of Ismael de Lugo, the senior priest in the invasion, addressed to the Cuban people, which Castro shared with the attending crowd. The Capuchin monk's appeal was primarily addressed to Cuban Catholics to let them know that the liberating army has arrived aiming to restore democratic

---

[12] CIA CS Historical Paper No. 105, 5 May, 1961. Web. 10 Aug. 2015.

[13] "*…un zarpazo traicionero del imperialismo…*" Discurso pronunciado por el Comandante Fidel Castro Ruz, Primer Ministro del Gobierno Revolucionario, en Ciudad Libertad, el 31 de diciembre de 1960. Web. 12 Aug. 2015.

[14] Discurso pronunciado por el Comandante Fidel Castro Ruz, Primer Ministro del Gobierno Revolucionario, resumiendo los actos del día internacional del trabajo. Plaza Cívica, 1° de mayo de 1961. Web. 12 Aug. 2015.

order in the country.[15] Castro's speech placed the emphasis entirely on the priests' foreign descent and falangist emotions; he separated them from the Cuban community simply on account of their origins and set them up as being in the service of American imperialism and the rich. The priests' involvement in the invasion caused the powers to take action; the Prime Minister also stated in his speech that the Revolutionary Government would issue a law banning foreign priests from the country. Only those would be allowed to stay in Cuba, with an additional license from the state, who haven't fought against the Revolution and haven't taken part in any counter-revolutionary activities. According to Castro, Church schools posed another problem as places where anti-revolutionary seeds were being sown into the souls of the youth, therefore, in the days to follow, the Revolutionary Government would nationalize private schools. Those owners with a proven decent and patriotic attitude toward the Revolution would be compensated, others, however, could not count on it. The teachers of secular private schools would receive work in state-maintained institutions. Religious education would only be permitted within church walls, but no churches would be closed down.[16] After the invasion, firm action was taken against the clergy; Evelio Díaz, Eduardo Boza Masvidal and many other priests were arrested, the *Actio Catolica* headquarters and some of the churches were temporarily closed down. Manuel Arteaga Betancourt, the Archbishop of Havana and Rodriguez Rosas, Bishop of Pinar del Río both, sought refuge from harassment at the Argentinian embassy (Castro Figueroa).

Based on Castro's speech, the powers seem to have turned more forcefully against the Catholic Church after the Bay of Pigs invasion and imparted a collective punishment to them for the active participation of the three chaplains. Castro's wrath seemed unappeasable. Nevertheless, the point of reference against the Church came in handy; with its help, he could remove the "foreign-hearted" priests from the country and force the upper clergy into silence. In his interview with the Mexican *Sucesos*

---

[15] Discurso pronunciado por el Comandante Fidel Castro Ruz, Primer Ministro del Gobierno Revolucionario, resumiendo los actos del día internacional del trabajo. Plaza Cívica, 1° de mayo de 1961. Web. 12 Aug. 2015.

[16] Ibidem.

magazine in 1966, he commented on the relationship between the State and the Church as well; the way he saw it then, "initially, the oligarchy has used the Catholic Church against the revolutionary changes", but now the Church is limited to its religious duties (IEPALA 33-34).[17] For this to happen within the span of a few years, the expulsion of the mainly foreign-born priests and nuns was a necessity. As a result, the number of priests remaining in Cuba had dropped to 220 by 1965 and nuns have all but disappeared from the island's life, only 190 of them continued to serve in the country (Jover Marimón 402). The clergy's, especially the nun's, departure in large numbers was closely related to the law pertaining to nationalization of private schools issued on the 6th of June, 1961,[18] as most of the teachers had come from their ranks.

Another incident associated with the Catholic community occurred in Havana on the 8th of September, during the celebration of the *Virgen de la Caridad del Cobre*. In the capital, the state permit issued for the two-day procession was withdrawn one day before the start of the festivities, then authorized again later for a different, early morning time. The organization of the procession was tied to the parish of Boza Masvidal, suffragan of Havana, as he was the priest of the *Nuestra Señora de la Caridad* parish. Many of the believers were not made aware of the changes, therefore, at least four thousand people have gathered for the procession to recall the celebration of the Blessed Mother and, at the same time, to protest the transpired events and the existing political situation. The Mexican *cristero* insurgency's well-known sentence, ¡*Viva Cristo Rey!* (Long live Christ the King) could also be heard among the chanted slogans. The parade was eventually broken up by the police, weapons were fired, one person died and several others were wounded as a circumstance. Two days after the incident, Boza Masvidal and numerous other priests who were deemed anti-regime have been arrested and exiled from Cuba on the 17th of September, 1961 aboard the Spanish ship, the *Covadonga* (Pedraza 107; Kirk 36).

---

[17] „La Iglesia Católica fue al principio utilizada por la oligarqía para combatir los cambios revolucionarios Quoted by IEPALA.

[18] Ley de Nacionalización general y gratuita de la enseñanza. 6 de junio de 1961. Web. 13 Aug. 2015.

The *Covadonga*, carrying the exiled priests, landed in the port of La Coruña in Spain, where its passengers received a solemn welcome. Boza Masvidal, suffragan bishop of Havana, told the press: "I left Cuba against my will" (Matovina and Poyo 171).

REFERENCES:

Blasier, Cole. "The Elimination of United States Influence." In: *Revolutionary Change in Cuba*. Ed. Carmelo Mesa-Lago. Pittsburgh: University of Pittsburgh Press, 1971. Print.

Boza Masdival, Eduardo. "Nuestro deber en el momento presente." In: *Historia eclesiástica de Cuba*. Ed. Ismael Testé. Barcelona: Consejo de Artes Gráficas Medinacelli S.A, 1975: 615-616. Print

The Cambridge History of Latin America. Vol. IV. C. 1870 to 1930. Ed. Leslie Bethell. Cambridge: Cambridge University Press, 1986. Print

Circular Colectiva del Episcopado Cubano. *Documentos de los obispos*: 60-62. Web. 2 Aug. 2015. http://profesorcastro.jimdo.com/la-jerarqu%C3%ADa cat% C3%B3lica-y-la-dictadura-de-batista/.

Castro Figueroa, Abel R. *Quo vadis, Cuba? Religión y Revolución*. Bloomington: CESJ, 2012. Print.

Cuba: A Short History. Ed. Leslie Bethell. Cambridge: Cambridge University Press, 1993. Print

Diario de la Marina, Cuban Catholic newspaper. Print.

Fernández, Damián J. *Cuba and the Politics of Passion*. Austin: University of Texas Press, 2000. Print.

Horváth, Emőke. "La iglesia católica cubana y el estado en 1959 según la circular *Vida Nueva*." *Acta Hispanica* 19 (2014): 27-37. Print.

IEPALA: *Las Relaciones Entre Cristianismo y Revolución: en Cuba, Tanzania, Nicaragua, Mozambique, El Salvador, Sudáfrica, Guatemala: Materiales Íntegros (ponencias, Diálogos e Informes del Trabajo en Grupos) del Encuentro sobre las Relaciones Entre Cristianismo y Revolución, Organizado por IEPALA en Madrid, del 5 al 12 de diciembre de 1981*. Madrid: IEPALA, 1982. 33-34. Print.

Jover Marimón, Mateo. "The Church." In: *Revolutionary Change in Cuba*. Ed. Carmelo Mesa-Lago, Pittsburgh: Pittsburgh University Press, 1974. Print.

Kirk, John. "La Iglesia en Cuba: ¿Emergiendo desde las catacumbas?" *Nueva Antropología*. 9.31 (1986): 23-48. Print.

Matovina, Timothy and Gerald E. Poyo, ¡Presente! U.S Latino Catholics from Colonial Origins to the Present. Maryknoll: Orbis, 2000. Print.

Pedraza, Silvia. Political Disaffection in Cuba's Revolution and Exodus. New York: Cambridge University Press, 2007. Print.

Pérez Serantes, Enrique. "Por Dios y por Cuba". In: Documentos de los obispos: 55-59. Web. http://profesorcastro.jimdo.com/la-jerarqu%C3%ADacat%C3%B3lica-y-la-dictadura-de-batista/.

Rabe, Stephen G. Eisenhower and Latin America. The Foreign Policy of Anticommunism. Chapel Hill: University of North Carolina Press, 1988: 166-176. Print.

Uría, Ignacio. Iglesia y revolución en Cuba. Enrique Pérez Serantes (1883-1868), el obispo que salvó a Fidel Castro. Madrid: Ediciones Encuentro, 2011. Print.

WILLIAM R. GLASS

Justifying American Interventionism: The 'Americans in Mexico' Westerns of the 1950s and 1960s

US foreign policy in the 1950s and 1960s faced a dilemma between people's popular perception of America's role in the world and the goals of their
political leaders. On the one hand, the popular myths of the US's revolutionary heritage of colonies rebelling for their independence produced
some sympathy for the wave of independence movements in European
colonies in Africa and Asia after World War II. On the other hand, with
the onset of the Cold War, US foreign policy became dominated by the
doctrine of containing communism. That goal was complicated by the
need to hold together an anti-communist alliance of western democracies which were in the process of suppressing rebellions in their colonies.
Those democracies often cast their suppression in terms of containment
to win American economic and military aid claiming that the rebels were
communists. In some cases that was true, as in Vietnam, but in many
places in Africa that was not the case (see Gaddis; Westad).

A subgenre of westerns[1] which I call "Americans in Mexico" in the first
two decades of the Cold War reveals a growing disillusionment with an

---

[1] Scholars have analyzed westerns as a film genre from a variety of perspectives, too volu-
minous to cover, but five scholars have influenced my thinking about westerns: Cawelti,
French, Lenihan, Slotkin (*Gunfighter Nation*), and Wright. All mention a variety of sub-

activist foreign policy of intervention designed to promote independence, freedom, and economic development. This trend evolved in this way: the earlier movies of the 1950s and early 1960s expressed the popular sentiment that US foreign policy should support the aspirations of people to find self-determination by freeing themselves from oppressive, exploitive dictators or governments and in so doing better their lives materially. Then, beginning in the mid-1960s, some of these movies offered a darker, more cynical commentary on US foreign policy. These films reflected the growing doubts about the Cold War consensus and the ability of the United States to defend democracy and promote capitalist development abroad in the name of containing communism.

Perhaps the most positive cinematic endorsement of American intervention is *The Magnificent Seven* (1960).[2] Though not set in one of Mexico's revolution, it is suggestive of the conditions that lead to revolution, does use the theme of commoners trying to free themselves from oppression, and reflects the optimism of the late 1950s and early 1960s about American engagement in economic development that would manifest itself in programs like the Peace Corps. Based on Akira Kurosawa's masterpiece, it tells the story of seven professional gunfighters who defend a poor Mexican village against the attacks of a gang of bandits. In particular, it affirms the ability of American foreign policy to intervene in the affairs of developing nations to bring about a more just society and improve the lives of the people. The policy of containment is implicit in the film's portrayal of the belief that improving the material and political circumstances of people would undercut the appeal of communist propaganda.

The mixture of motives which the seven give for joining the mission is one of the best ways to see this positive justification of American foreign

---

genres and plot conventions and discuss films studied here, but none isolate the generic conventions I describe or analyze the films as a commentary on interventionism. French is the most political, categorizing westerns according to presidential styles. Slotkin's work is the most comprehensive, while Cawelti, Lenihan, and Wright focus on post-World War II westerns and their connection to social change in the United States.

[2] This reading of *The Magnificent Seven* has been shaped, in part, by Slotkin, "Gunfighters and Green Berets." For a detailed discussion of the production, see Lovell, Chapter 11 "Seven the Hard Way."

policy. What is interesting is that only one of the seven (Harry, played by Brad Dexter) sees this opportunity as a chance to enrich himself. He is convinced that the job is more than just "shooing flies away from a village," that cattle or a payroll or conquistador gold and silver or Aztec treasure will be the ultimate reward.[3] The rest of the seven express personal reasons that broadly suggest a lack of interest in economic profit that could come from their intervention. This point is made as all reject the offered pay of twenty dollars and room and board. This is not to suggest that economic considerations are absent. Three of the seven are broke, and the job thus becomes something to tide them over until a more lucrative opportunity comes along. After first rejecting the offer, the knife-wielding Britt (James Coburn) changes his mind and joins the seven because he is attracted by the competition and the danger; the job is a chance to test his skills.

Chris (Yul Brynner) and Chico (Horst Buchholz) represent the characters with the most complex motives. Though he may be a mercenary, Chris acts out his own sense of justice and ideals. When three Mexican villagers ask for his help in buying guns, Chris suggests that they hire men because "men are cheaper than guns." But he resists signing on – "I'm not in the blessing business" – until he hears the story of the village. Tomás, Hilario, and Miguel explain that their village is too small for the Mexican government to garrison troops there to protect it but it could be a good place to live if they could keep the resources their village produces instead of losing it to marauding bandits. Also, Chris is impressed by their commitment to see the job through to its completion. To see if they are worthy of American intervention, he warns them, "Once you begin, you have to be prepared for killing and more killing, and still more killing until the reason for it is gone". Hilario affirms that all the men the village will fight.

Chico, on the other hand, is a character that suggests the policy makers' assumption that the basic aspiration of developing nations to remake themselves in the image of America. He is a Mexican from a village not all that different from the one the seven pledge to protect. He has the clothes, guns, and desire to be a gunfighter like the rest of seven, but

---

[3] All quotations of dialog from the films are my transcriptions of them from the respective DVDs.

seems to lack the skill. He fails Chris's quick draw test, and this failure reflects a more serious problem with American military assistance. It is not enough to provide guns and technology but American expertise and advisors are also necessary. At one point, the ineptness of the villagers in using pistols and rifles leads O'Reilly to shout in frustration at Miguel, "Don't shoot the gun, . . . use it like a club". But this incompetence is what Chico wants to escape, and joining the seven is Chico's way of proving that he has separated himself from the villagers.

This interpretation of the seven's motives of disinterested benevolence is reinforced by the contrast with Calvera (Eli Wallach), the leader of the bandit gang terrorizing the village. Calvera's politics are never clearly spelled out. His words and actions do not mark him as a communist; he is more of a paternalistic dictator who runs his gang with an authoritarian hand. Ironically, then, he is the kind of leader US foreign policy often supported during the 1950s and 1960s as a bulwark against communism. Thus in a curious way, because the seven support the villagers over Calvera, the movie offers a fairly pointed critique of the policy of backing exploitive dictators in the name of containing communism. The contrast with the seven is sharply drawn. In the first confrontation with the seven, Calvera tells them "We're in the same business". To which Vin replies, "Only as competitors". Calvera then asks Chris if he would like to become partners and adds the line that reveals the most about his view of the villagers: "If God didn't want them sheared, he would not have made them sheep". By this point in the story, the seven have become enmeshed in the life of the village. Some have considered the possibility of retiring to the village. Furthermore, the seven are bound by their sense of duty; they have taken a contract and will honor it. So Chris rejects Calvera's offer of a partnership by telling him to "ride on!"

Even after the villagers welcome Calvera back, the seven return in order to fulfill their contract. Calvera's explanation of why the villagers betrayed the seven also highlights a key problem of building democracy in developing nations: "Your friends, they don't like you much anymore," he tells Chris. "You force them to make too many decisions. With me, there is only one decision: do what I say". Calvera lets the seven leave because he fears that if he kills them their friends will take revenge on him.

But they decide to make one last attempt to free the village, even if the villagers do not want this freedom. Here, again, the mixture of motives is revealing. By this point, Harry has concluded that there is nothing of value in the village and hence no reason for him to join in what he sees as a suicide mission. For Britt, Calvera's actions are a personal affront to Britt's sense of honor, while Lee sees an opportunity for personal redemption. Chris, Vin, and O'Reilly have come to value the peaceful life of the village and want to give it a chance to flourish. Chico is ambivalent. He hates Calvera and what Calvera has done to the village but he is hurt and embarrassed by the villagers' betrayal and wonders if the sacrifice will be worth the effort. On the other hand, he is alienated from the rest of the seven not just by his ethnicity but also by the realization that it is not only men like Calvera who have turn the villagers into sheep but also men like the seven.

The result of the seven's attack is the village's freedom. In a nineteenth century western version of a surgical strike or precision bombing, the seven ambush Calvera's men while sparing the villagers, who join in the battle with their hoes, axes, machetes, shovels, and stools. Interestingly, the first to die is Harry, even the greediest American can act selflessly on occasion. Thus the seven are victorious, and the village emancipated from Calvera's authoritarianism, vindicating a policy of armed intervention. While the villagers are grateful, they are also glad to see the surviving American gunslingers leave. The old man tells Chris and Vin, "they wouldn't be sorry to see you stay, you know." "Yes," Chris replies, "but they won't be sorry to see us go, either". This dialogue seems to suggest American motives and intervention will always be under a certain degree of suspicion. Only Chico remains, rejecting the way of the gun for the life of a farmer.

Hollywood's fascination with Mexican revolutions reached a climax in the years around 1970, years in which revolutions, political, cultural, and social, seemed to be everywhere. Nine movies set in revolutionary Mexico were released in the years 1968-1972. Bookended with movies about Pancho Villa, these movies span the spectrum from suggesting the positive contribution American intervention could make to the comic incompetence of the US military. But the best of the lot and the most pessimistic and cynical in assessing the value of American intervention is Sam Peckinpah's *The Wild Bunch* (1969).[4]

Critics (and scholars) should respect Peckinpah's explicit denial of a political message in *The Wild Bunch*. In an interview, Peckinpah commented "I wasn't trying to make an epic, I was trying to tell a simple story about bad men in changing times" (qtd. in Farber 8). But later he acknowledged that "the western is a universal frame within which it is possible to comment on today" (qtd. in Bliss 36). Moreover, he chose to situate the story of *The Wild Bunch* in a specific time and place. The themes of the passing of the frontier and loyalty to one's comrades could have worked in a setting, say, two decades earlier in the 1890s when Frederick Jackson Turner proclaimed the frontier closed. Setting the story in 1913 in the early years of the Mexican Revolution – a decade and a half after America's splendid little war to liberate Cuba, on the eve of America's intervention in the Great War to make the world safe for democracy, and most tellingly right before American troops literally go into Mexico – legitimates a more political analysis of Peckinpah's film.[5]

Though, in many ways, a more complex and ambitious film than almost all of the films in the Americans in Mexico genre, *The Wild Bunch* may be simpler to analyze as a commentary on the policy of intervention. At one level, the movie suggests that the motive for American intervention is nothing more than greed. Pike (William Holden) confesses, "Ain't getting around any better. I'd like to make one good score and back off". The opportunity for that payoff comes when Mapache (Emilio Fernandez) hires the bunch to steal a shipment of arms from the US Army. It is here that a comparison with the seven reveals a sugarcoating in Sturges's film that makes *The Wild Bunch*'s critique of American foreign policy the more incisive. Where it was an overlooked subtext in *The Magnificent Seven*,

---

[4] Of the three directors, Peckinpah has received the most critical attention. See Weddle and Fine for biography and discussion of the productions of Peckinpah's films. Dukore and Fulwood contextualize Peckinpah's western in a discussion of his complete filmography while Seydor focuses on just the westerns.

[5] For a different assessment of the political content of *The Wild Bunch*, see Sharrett 79-104. Some scholars have noted the connections to Vietnam. See, for example, French who described the film as "a rather obvious and bitter allegory about Vietnam."

or more accurately, a deliberately obscured reality, the true nature of the Americans who go into Mexico is explicit in *The Wild Bunch*. For all their nobility, the seven are not that different from the bunch; they are men who make their living by their guns. The seven may not have crossed over to the other side of the law, but they are on the border, literally and figuratively. While the seven reject Calvera's offer of partnership, Dutch (Ernest Borgnine) suggests of Mapache, "Generalissimo, hell! He's just another bandit grabbing all he can for himself". Pike accepts this characterization and applies it to the bunch: "Like some others I could mention". Moreover, the bunch is not a democracy, but neither is the seven nor the professionals. Pike is clearly in command of the bunch and the rest are expected to follow his lead. At one point he asserts, "I either lead this bunch or end it right now". Interestingly Chris of the seven maintains his authority over the villagers. Though he affirms that the seven work for the villagers, as he watches their debate over continuing to fight Calvera, he warns them, "I'll kill the first man who talks of giving up." This is hardly a lesson in democratic choice.

Analyzing how the final shootout comes about reveals a different, more subtle level to *The Wild Bunch*'s critique of the policy of intervention or more precisely it raises the question of the cost of that intervention. As the bunch flees the bounty hunters chasing them after their failed robbery in the opening set piece, Angel (Jamie Sanchez) takes them to his village in Mexico. There, the bunch are startled to find that they are accepted and respected, even though the villagers are well aware of who they are and what they do. Portrayed as an idyll, the verdant green of the trees is in sharp contrast to the arid desert through which the bunch has been traveling and to Mapache's headquarters in Aqua Verde, which is anything but green. Moreover, Peckinpah presents a certain innocence about the village that is reinforced by a discussion between the village elder and Pike. As children skinny-dip in a stream in the background, they watch Angel as he anguishes over his girlfriend becoming Mapache's mistress. The elder observes, "We all dream of being a child again, even the worst of us, perhaps the worst most of all". The irony here is that throughout the film Peckinpah shows the innocence of children is a myth, the evil that the Bunch and Mapache represent is but the natural manifestation of a tendency deeply rooted in human nature: the children torturing scorpions during the opening credits, the children in the mayhem as the bunch is ambushed during their escape from robbing the train office, the children reenacting this gunfight in its aftermath, the baby's clinched fist on the bandolier worn by its mother while it suckles at her breast, the admiration of the young boy for Mapache, children riding on Angel's back as he is tortured; these images culminate in a boy killing Pike by shooting him in the back.

Like the seven, then, the bunch sees in the village a different way of life, one that is free from guns but also one that needs to be defended because it is threatened. They learn that Mapache's men have recently raided the village, stealing horses, cattle, and corn and killing seven, two by hanging. Among the dead was Angel's father. Holding one of the bunch's rifles, the elder expresses his belief that they would have been able to defend themselves had they had this technology. This explains why Dutch rejects Pike's identification with Mapache: "We ain't nothing like him; we don't hang people". Significantly and fatefully, he adds, "I hope someday these people here kick him and the rest of the scum like him right into their graves". And Angel agrees, "We will, if it takes forever". So it is that the bunch agrees to let Angel take a case of rifles in lieu of his share of the gold Mapache agrees to pay them for stealing the arms. They tell Mapache that one of the cases was lost but the ruse is discovered and Mapache takes and tortures Angel. Disgusted by the scene, Pike and Dutch convince the Gorch brothers they should rescue Angel because "when you side with a man you stay with him. If you can't you like some animal. You're finished, we're finished, all of us!" The motivation, then, that leads to the final battle is more personal and tied to the bunch's own code of honor and loyalty rather than a sense of duty to protect the village. But the results are the same: Mapache and his army are destroyed and Angel's village is freed, but at a tremendous price. The bunch are dead and so are many innocents.

America's perception of the good that it could accomplish by intervening in the affairs of other nations underwent a radical shift in the 1960s. To say it was due in no small measure to its experiences in Vietnam might be something of an oversimplification, but it would not be far from the truth. Domestic developments should not be overlooked, though. Generational confrontation, conflict over civil rights for African-Americans, and changing roles for women in society shook the consensus concerning the ideals by which Americans lived. Moreover, the violence of these years – the race riots, the assassinations, the daily body counts from Vietnam – seemed to reveal a darker side to America. Of these three films, *The Magnificent Seven* offers the most positive assessment of American intervention, even if there was an unacknowledged darker underside to the story. Made and released in 1960, it shows American intervention bringing peace and security, affirming Americans' belief in their nation's ability to effect positive change in developing nations. By mid-1960, doubts were creeping in. John Kennedy had been assassinated, Watts had gone up in flames, students began protesting the conduct of the war in Vietnam, and most importantly, Senator J. William Fulbright had offered a scathing critique of the policy of intervention, denouncing it as an exercise in the "arrogance of power." Appearing in theaters in the summer of 1969, when barely 30 per cent of Americans thought sending troops to Vietnam was a good policy (Lunch and Sperlich), *The Wild Bunch* reflected the public's disillusionment with an activist foreign policy by laying bare American interventionism's avarice and destructiveness. After Peckinpah's film, Hollywood's interest in Mexico's revolution as means of commentary on intervention waned, but legacy of these films provide not only a picture of the shifting evaluation of the policy of intervention during the 1960s but also a conversion that the United States could revisit.

REFERENCES:

The Magnificent Seven. Dir. John Sturges. The Mirsch Corporation. 1960. DVD.

The Wild Bunch. Dir. Sam Peckinpah. Warner Bros. 1969. DVD.

Bliss, Michael. "Martyred Slaves of Time: Age, Regret, and Transcendence in *The Wild Bunch*." In: *Peckinpah Today: New Essays on the Films of Sam Peckinpah*. Ed. Michael Bliss. Carbondale: Southern Illinois University Press, 2012. Print.

Cawelti, John G. *The Six-Gun Mystique*. 2nd ed. Bowling Green: Bowling Green State University Popular Press, 1984. Print.

Dukore, Bernard F. *Sam Peckinpah's Feature Films*. Urbana: University of Illinois Press, 1999. Print.

Farber, Stephen. "Peckinpah's Return." *Film Quarterly* 23.1 (1969): 2-11. Web. 24 Oct. 2013.

Fine, Marshall. *Bloody Sam: The Life and Films of Sam Peckinpah*. New York: Miramax Books, 2005. Print.

French, Philip. *Westerns: Aspects of a Movie Genre*. London: Secker and Walberg, 1973. Rpt. in *Westerns*. Manchester: Carcanet Press, 2005. Kindle file.

Fulbright, J. William. "The Arrogance of Power." Typescript. J. William Fulbright Papers. Special Collections, University of Arkansas Libraries. Web. 24 Sep. 2015.

Fulwood, Neil. *The Films of Sam Peckinpah*. London: Batsford, 2003. Kindle file.

Gaddis, John Lewis. *The Cold War: A New History*. New York: Penguin Books, 2005. Print.

Lenihan, John H. *Showdown: Confronting Modern America in the Western Film*. Urbana: University of Illinois Press, 1985. Print.

Lovell, Glenn. *Escape Artist: The Life and Films of John Sturges*. Madison: The University of Wisconsin Press, 2008. Kindle file.

Lunch, William L. and Peter W. Sperlich. "Public Opinion and the Vietnam War." *The Western Political Science Quarterly* 32.1 (1979): 21-44. Web. 17 Oct. 2008.

Seydor, Paul. *Peckinpah: The Western Films*. Urbana: University of Illinois Press, 1980. Print.

Sharrett, Christopher. "Peckinpah the Radical: The Politics of *The Wild Bunch*." In: *Sam Peckinpah's The Wild Bunch*. Ed. Stephen Prince. Cambridge: Cambridge University Press, 1999: 79-104. Print.

Slotkin, Richard. *Gunfighter Nation: The Myth of the Frontier in Twentieth-Century America*. Norman: University of Oklahoma Press, 1988. Print.

—. "Gunfighters and Green Berets: The Magnificent Seven and the Myth of Counter-Insurgency." *Radical History Review* (Spring 1989): 65-90. Rpt. in *Hollywood's America: United States History through Its Films*. Ed. Steven Mintz, Randy Roberts. St. James, NY: Brandywine Press, 1993: 231-41. Print.

Weddle, David. *"If They Move… Kill 'Em!": The Life and Times of Sam Peckinpah*. New York: Grove Press, 1994. Print.

Westad, Odd Arne. *The Global Cold War: Third World Interventions and the Making of Our Times*. Cambridge: Cambridge University, 2007. Kindle file.

Wright, Will. *Sixguns and Society: a Structural Study of the Western*. Berkeley: University of California Press, 1975. Print.

KRISZTINA MAGYAR

Womb and Breasts: Female Body Parts in Seventeenth-Century Puritan Political Communications

During the 1630s, many Puritans felt compelled to leave England and settle on the other side of the Atlantic. Threatened by a possible return of the Church of England, now reformed along Calvinist lines, to Catholicism in the wake of William Laud's religious policies, these people left despite their deep loyalty to it. They strongly opposed religious separatism and understood the New England venture as physical relocation without institutional separation. As the years in New England progressed, they continued to uphold this stance even as they had created their own church polity that made the differences between Old and New England rather more than less obvious.

It should be noted that the Puritan migration to the New World and the innovations in ecclesiastical polity took place in a religious and political climate in which mainstream Reformers held a responsible attitude to the maintenance of church unity. I.W.C. van Wyk, for example, speaks of a "general attitude of loyalty and camaraderie between all people who identified with the renewal movements" (Wyk 217). With reference to the Puritans, Abram C. Van Engen contends that "in the wider transatlantic world of the 1630s and 1640s," they thought of themselves as "bound together by a special love of brethren and fighting together for a wider reformation" (Van Engen 118).

In this climate, the emigrants' behavior was met with fear and resentment by many of their co-religionists, who repeatedly confronted them with charges of abandonment and schism. In the early years of settlement, New England clergy was frequently called upon, through correspondence, to answer questions from England concerning colonial church polity; the vigorous debates between New Englanders and the godly back at home that characterized these early years kept the issue of religious separatism firmly on the agenda.

In 1630, Puritan minister John Cotton preached a farewell sermon to John Winthrop's departing fleet in Southampton. In the sermon, entitled "Gods Promise to his Plantation," Cotton exhorted the company to continue to be "present in spirit" with the godly who were to remain at home, "though absent in body." The emigrating party was not to unmindfull," in the New World, of the national church that they were now to leave behind. "Forget not the wombe that bare you, and the breasts that gave you sucke," Cotton instructed the departing company. When Cotton preached this sermon, apparently he was well aware of the danger that the emigrating party might confuse the literal with the metaphorical: he warned that departure from England could *not* mean departure from the church. He underlined the need for a continuing "amity and unity of brethren" despite the fact that something as extensive as the Atlantic Ocean was from then on to divide the two parties (Cotton b 18-19).

A few months later, Cotton penned a letter to Samuel Skelton, minister of the Salem church in Massachusetts.[1] In the letter, Cotton warned Skelton against religious separatism using almost the same words that he had used in his sermon to Winthrop's party in Southampton: "Reject not the womb that bare you, nor the paps that gave you suck" (Cotton c 57). Cotton added that the Salem church was not to withdraw from the Church of England until Christ gave them "a bill of divorcement" (Cotton c 57).

The image that Cotton used to warn of separatism recurs in at least two documents whose purpose was to refute accusations that New Englanders

---

[1] Skelton left England in 1629, so his departure preceded the major flow of Puritans during the 1630s. Salem, where he became minister, was an already existing English settlement.

had begun to turn their backs on the English church. In 1635 Cotton, by this time not only an emigrant himself but the leading spokesman for the congregational way, wrote a letter to a minister in England,[2] in answer to accusations that New Englanders had renounced communion with the Anglican Church. In the letter Cotton asserted that

> … we willingly and thankefully acknowledge, and do professe, that the hope which most of us have obtained of the common salvation we received from the preaching of Gods faithfull Ministers among you, wee cannot, we dare not deny to Blesse the Wombe which bare us, and the Paps which gave us sucke … (Cotton a 3)

Church-Government and Church-Covenant Discussed, in which Richard Mather replied a series of questions from a group of English ministers concerning New England church polity, employs the same imagery.[3] In one place Mather declares that New Englanders have *not* renounced the English church for her impurities. Then he adds, "…. nor can we judge or speake harshly of the Wombes[4] that bare us, nor of the paps which gave us suck" (Mather 29).

In fact, the womb and breasts co-occur in the Bible several times. An example can be found in Gen. 49:25 ("blessings of the breasts and the womb"), which, according to Craig A. Evans, is paraphrased in *Targum Neofiti* as "Blessed are the breasts from which you sucked and the womb within which you lay" (Evans 255). In the Gospel of Luke, they occur in two beatitudes, in 11:27 and in 23:29. In the first instance, they are put for Jesus' mother, in the second, for women in general. Luke 11:27 reads: "And it came to pass, as he spake these things, a certain woman of the company lifted up her voice, and said unto him, Blessed is the womb that bare thee, and the paps which thou hast sucked."

---

[2] According to Susan Hardman Moore, the minister was someone from the Stour Valley. See Moore. Composition of the letter predates its publication in 1641.

[3] Mather compiled these replies sometime during the 1630s. They were printed with this title in 1643, together with two other manuscripts. See Moore.

[4] Use of the plural in this passage is interesting. "Wombes" refers to particular congregations within the Church of England.

The exact opposite of what the woman said in Luke 11:27 is announced by Jesus in 23:29: "For, behold, the days are coming, in the which they shall say, Blessed are the barren, and the wombs that never bare, and the paps which never gave suck."[5]

The two Lukan beatitudes invert the order in which the two female body parts appear in Gen. 49:25 and its targumic paraphrase. Furthermore, in 11:27, the woman attributes agency to the womb, though not to the breasts. In Luke's second beatitude, agency, albeit frustrated, is attributed both to the womb and to the breasts.

The formula that Cotton and Mather use closely resembles Luke's two blessings. Importantly, the Puritan divines represent the womb and the breasts as active agents. But while in Luke the body parts stand for the whole person, mother or woman, Cotton and Mather make a further imaginative leap and make them stand for the Church of England. The original declarations of blessedness become either injunctions ("forget not," "reject not"), in the documents composed in England, or declarations of the inability to deny or to be too critical of the Church of England, in the documents composed in New England.

Use of the synecdoche instead of a simple reference to the Anglican Church as a mother results in her becoming emphatically embodied. Her maternity is not an abstraction but concrete and tangible. Furthermore, as we have seen, the two female body parts are active agents and not inert instruments that an infant uses: they "bear" (give birth) and "give suck."

Cotton and Mather, in conceptualizing their national church not simply as a mother but as an anatomical compound made up of a womb and breasts, adopted Calvin's imagistic understanding of the visible church. In the *Institutes* Calvin explains that God collects his children into the bosom of the church, not only to be nourished by her in their infancy and childhood, but also to "be guided by her maternal care until they grow up to manhood, and, finally, attain to the perfection of faith." He adds further that "to those to whom he [God] is a Father, the Church must also be a mother" (Calvin b 622-623).

---

[5] Both the Geneva Bible and the Authorized King James Version, two important bibles for the Puritans, render the two Lukan blessings in this way.

Calvin emphasizes that, "from her single title of Mother," it is both useful and necessary to know her,

> since there is no other means of entering into life unless she conceive us in the womb and give us birth, unless she nourish us at her breasts, in short, keep us under her charge and government, until, divested of mortal flesh, we become like the angels (Mt. 22:30). (Calvin b 625)

Furthermore, in his commentary on Ephesians 4:12, Calvin writes, "The Church is truly the common mother of all believers, and in the Lord begets kings as well as simple citizens, nourishes and governs them" (Nijenhuis 1994: 37). In Calvin's understanding, it is a Christian's duty to cultivate unity with the church as "the mother of all the godly" (Calvin b: 621). Departure from it "is always fatal" (Calvin b: 625). Calvin's catechism also warns that those who "rend its unity by faction, are cut off from all hope of salvation during the time they remain in this schism, be it however short" (Calvin a).

Following Calvin, the two Puritan divines zoomed in on the womb and breasts and attributed agency to them in order to highlight the active role that the Anglican Church had played in the formation of their identity as a religious community, educating them and promoting their social cohesion. In 1630, Cotton warned both Winthrop's departing company and Samuel Skelton in New England not to forget what the institutional church had done for them. In the same manner, Cotton and Mather, in the documents that they compiled in New England, acknowledged indebtedness of this kind. However, representing the Anglican Church in such emphatically corporeal terms enabled non-separating New England Puritans, in whose name Cotton and Mather spoke when they defended the New England cause, not only to profess their vital connectedness to their first origins but also, at the same time, to make claims to some difference. After all, differentiation is what made the New England venture meaningful. Serene Jones points out that the image of the womb and breasts establishes difference "through substantial, enfleshed interactions" (Jones 28). Between the bodies of mother and child, "there is a constant exchange of fluid and blood across the boundaries dividing them" (Jones 28). Jones argues that the line between the two bodies does exist but the boundaries are blurred. In the womb and in nursing, "the task of attaining definition and distinction takes second place to the more primordial task of discovering the security of connection ..." (Jones 28).[6]

Relating what Jones says about natural mothering to the New England experiment and understanding it metaphorically in this context, we can say that if a mother's womb and breasts are so powerful in blurring boundaries between otherwise two distinct bodies, then the synecdoche is an apt trope in political communications whose aim is precisely to smooth over differences and physical separateness and to affirm connectedness. The emigrants felt constrained not only by traditional notions of loyalty and obligation to the Anglican Church, but also by Calvinism's understanding of the visible church as the common mother of the godly, departure from which was understood to be fatal for the believer. Cotton obviously found the synecdoche an apt device to remind both Winthrop's party and Samuel Skelton of their duty of continuing allegiance. However, as an emigrant, Cotton also found it useful, along with Mather, to use it in correspondence that had the aim to assure the godly at home of New Englanders' continuing communion with the English church, but which, at the same time, made claims to autonomy as regarded the constitution of New England churches. In fact, first-generation New England Puritans found themselves in a liminal position: while they were physically relocated and had their own way of constituting churches, they still thought of themselves as thoroughly English, as a community of the godly who continued to be bound by a thousand ties to the country and church that they had left behind.

However, the metaphorical mother, while allowing for distance and difference, not only imposed a duty of connection, a duty, if neglected, threatened spiritual destruction, but also provided the "the security of connection" that Jones speaks about. No doubt that the need for such

---

[6] I have applied Jones' insights to my topic from an essay of hers in which she contrasts two different theological traditions of rendering God's relationship to the world, the mother-child and the covenantal or contractual relationship, and in which she discusses why conceptualizing God as a mother – with a womb, breasts and arms – and not as a legal partner makes all the difference. Jones.

security was acutely felt in the early years of settlement. Considering the fact that the Puritans who emigrated became separated from friends and were deprived of the comforts of living and the physical security they had been accustomed to in their homeland, migration must have imposed a heavy physical and psychological burden upon them all. The Puritans who left for the New World were not people with nothing to lose. When Cotton told the godly at home that New Englanders both could not and dared not deny to bless the womb and breasts of the Church of England, he not only acknowledged New Englanders' awareness of what they owed her as parent,[7] but also gave voice to the anxiety of destruction (in every sense of the word) in the name of many of the colonists.

References:

Calvin, John (a). *Catechism of the Church of Geneva*. Web. http://www.reformed. org/documents/calvin/geneva_catachism/geneva_catachism.html.

Calvin, John (b). *Institutes of the Christian Religion*. Transl. Henry Beveridge. Grand Rapids, MI: Christian Classics Ethereal Library, 2002. Web. http:// www.ccel.org/ccel/calvin/institutes.html.

Cotton, John (a). *A copy of a letter of Mr. Cotton of Boston, in New England, sent in answer of certain objections made against their discipline and orders there, directed to a friend...* [London]: [s.n.], 1641. Web. http://quod.lib.umich. edu/e/eebo/A34672.0001.001/1:2?rgn=div1;view=fulltext.

Cotton, John (b). "Gods Promise to His Plantation." Web. http://digitalcom mons.unl.edu/cgi/viewcontent.cgi?article=1022&context=etas.

Cotton, John (c). [Letter to Samuel Skelton], Boston, 2 Oct. 1630. Reprinted in: Harris, Thaddeus Mason. *Memorials of the First Church in Dorchester: From its Settlement in New England to the End of the second Century: in Two Discourses, Delivered July 4, 1830*. Boston: from the Office of the Daily Advertiser, 1830: 53-57.

---

[7] Apparently, both Cotton and Mather conceptualized the Church of England as a godly mother who breastfed her own children instead of putting them in the care of a wet-nurse. Equally apparently, they conceptualized New Englanders' obligations to the church in terms of godly children's duty of reverence to their parents, a duty commanded in the Bible. For a discussion of the Puritan advocacy of maternal breastfeeding over wet-nursing in the period, see, for example, Trubowitz.

Engen, Abram C. Van. *Sympathetic Puritans: Calvinist Fellow Feeling in Early New England.* New York: Oxford University Press, 2005. Print.

Evans, Craig A. *The Bible Knowledge Commentary: Matthew-Luke*, Vol. 1. Colorado Springs, CO: Cook Communication Ministries, 2003. Print.

Jones, Serene. "Glorious Creation, Beautiful Law." In: *Feminist and Womanist Essays in Reformed Dogmatics.* Columbia Series in Reformed Theology. Eds. Amy Plantinga Pauw and Serene Jones. Louisville: Westminster John Knox Press, 2006. Print.

Mather, Richard. *Church Government and Church Covenant Discussed.* Reprinted by Quinta Press. Weston Rhyn, 2008. Web. http://quintapress.macmate.me/PDF_Books/Church_Government_and_Covenant.pdf.

Moore, Susan Hardman. *Pilgrims: New World Settlers & the Call of Home.* New Haven [Conn.]; London: Yale University Press, 2007. Print.

Nijenhuis, Willem. *Ecclesia Reformata: Studies on the Reformation*, Vol. 2. Leiden: Brill, 1994. Print.

The quotes from the Gospel of Luke are taken from the *Authorized King James Version* (Oxford: Oxford University Press, 2008).

Trubowitz, Rachel. *Nation and Nurture in Seventeenth-Century English Literature.* Oxford: Oxford University Press, 2012. Print.

Wyk, I.W.C. van. "Calvin, Luther and Church Unity." *In die Skriflig 44* Supplement 3 (2010): 215-231. Web. http://www.indieskriflig.org.za/index.php/skriflig/article/viewFile/190/86.

All of the internet sources used in this paper were checked for their availability and reliability on 28 Sep., 2015.

IRÉN ANNUS

From Mollywood with Humor:
A Mormon *Pride and Prejudice*

HUMOR AND RELIGION

"Humor and religion are not the best of friends" (Capps 413). A number of studies on the Christian attitude to laughter seem to support this statement. Saroglou finds that "the mistrust towards the comic in early Christianity seems to be based on the need for control. ... Emotions are viewed with suspicion because of their unpredictable character... [and] as a failure of self-mastery" (Saroglou 201). He points to Gregory of Nyssa, the fourth-century bishop, as already having regarded "laughter as an enemy of man, because laughter is neither a word nor action ordered towards any possible goal" (Saroglou 196). He also argues (Saroglou 194) that the need for definite answers and a coherent worldview with limited uncertainties are also fundamental to religions – and humor, by its very nature, challenges this attitude, which is yet another possible reason for the contempt leveled at it.

In his study of the history of humor in Christianity, Morreall finds that the most powerful "condemnations of laughter came from monastic leaders" (Morreall 273). He locates the origin of this dominant attitude in the rules of St. Benedict from 529, which have become a standard in Western monasticism. "Benedict proposed a 'Ladder of Humility' on which Step

Ten was a restraint against laughter, and Step Eleven a warning against joking" (Morreall 217). Morreall explains the Christian condemnation of laughter and humor that also appeared outside of monastic orders by the fact that "religions are based on certain beliefs, values and rituals, deemed worthy of absolute respect. Each religion requires of its followers a commitment to these ... which is incompatible with taking a humorous or playful attitude toward them" (Morreall 230).

Le Goff, on the other hand, relates the monastic restrictions on humor to the process of successful religious indoctrination. He observes that humor could represent a form of intellectual challenge to the strict logic of the uniform dogma that monks were to adhere to along with the absolute authority and resultant power the establishment imposed on their followers. This also means that humor was regarded as a possible means through which this authority could be not only questioned and debated, but also undermined and subverted. This is confirmed by Capps' point that "religion is associated with a need for control ... [along with] orderliness, conscientiousness, and low impulsivity" (Le Goff 429), all of which provided further reasons for a general resentment of humor.

These studies demonstrate that humor has traditionally been regarded as possessing an unusual potential for questioning, challenging, and even possibly subverting religious beliefs, practices, and worldviews. This fear of humor has been a particular concern for young churches and highly conservative communities, where anxieties about denominational growth or the perhaps overtly serious attitude and strict nature of religious practice account for the heightened resentment of humor in general. The ability of a community not only to tolerate humor that expresses a form of criticism of one's faith and denomination, but also to generate witty and creative self-referential humor, thus, may be interpreted as a sign that a young denomination, such as Mormonism, has come of age, feeling comfortable and self-assured, both in its faith and in its place in American society.

I argue that the adaptation of Jane Austen's *Pride and Prejudice* produced in 2003 in Mollywood – the popular term for Mormon filmmaking – is an example of this self-referential Mormon humor. The movie was originally designed exclusively for Mormon or Latter-day Saint (LDS) spectators, but was also found appropriate for a broader audience, since – as Wells and Annus propose – the movie crosses over periods, forms of media, religions, and nations. In addition, the attitude with which the LDS Church has responded to other representations of the Saints in American mainstream popular culture, such as the highly acclaimed musical *The Book of Mormon* (2012), also demonstrates that the Saints have realized that "humor, paradoxically, may support a culture at the same time that it subverts it" (Heddendorf xvi).

HUMOR AND MORMONISM IN AMERICAN SOCIETY

"The comic is a celebration of the contradictions of human life, such as those between effort and result, capacity and ambition, intention and external accident (Hegel), expectation and disappointment (Kant), life and matter (Bergson), and the experience of both being and possessing a body (Plessner)" (Saroglou 193). Davies observes that the logic of humor typically allows for people in the center to be the ones "laughing at people at the periphery" (Davies 1), exaggerating differences constituted on the basis of gender, race, and religion, among other areas. Jokes tend to portray groups on the margins from the majority perspective, establishing practices of representation that contribute to the maintenance of social hierarchies, dominant ideologies, and hegemonic power structures.

Mormonism has been portrayed in this fashion in the United States from its inception in 1830. Perhaps the most widely known visual critic of Mormonism was Thomas Nast, the outstanding cartoonist of the 19th century. He used the figure of a turtle-like reptile to symbolize the Mormon Church, representing it as an undesirable social body, unfit for American freedom and democracy. Mormon portrayals in the Anglo-American literature of the age have been investigated by Austin, who concludes that they were depicted as a frontier community associated with "lawlessness, chaos, and sexual promiscuity." This stereotypical representation, he contends, has changed since then, and the Saints are now portrayed rather as "hyperobedient, patriotic, conservative, and, in all probability, sexually repressed." A volume edited by Decker and Austin in 2010 surveys the portrayal of Mormonism in contemporary American popular culture. It demonstrates the changing nature of humor and stereotypes with which the Saints are currently treated, indicating that now the missionary figure seems to be the central trope in these productions.

In parallel, notes Baker, Mormon in-group humor also evolved, and started to appear in print in the post-World War II period. Wilson in particular has investigated Mormon jokes: he has found that they are relatively new and target "the beleaguered bishop, his counterpart, the Relief Society president ... leaders at lower levels of authority" (Wilson 8), to which each Saint can relate through personal experience. Cannon finds that, in a broader sense, humor within the LDS community "helps defuse sensitive subjects such as sex as well as latent resentment toward the Church's authoritarian and sometimes autocratic power structure" (Cannon 19). She notes that they also "crave respectability and credibility" (20) from the wider society which prevents them from using more humor. I suggest that the series of comedies that Mollywood has recently started to produce may thus be interpreted as a sign of change in this regard.

MORMON HUMOR IN *PRIDE AND PREJUDICE*

Pride and Prejudice was the first movie directed and produced by Scottish director Andrew Black, who moved to the US and converted to Mormonism as an adult. The script was co-written by his wife, Anne Black, also a Saint, and was entitled *Pride and Prejudice: A Utah Comedy*. With this original title retained, the movie immediately took its place in the series of Austen adaptations so popular at the turn of the century (Annus; Tóth). While the final version of the movie was shown without the subtitle and with specifically Mormon sections omitted – in the belief that it would appeal to a wider audience – it does include a series of references and images that undoubtedly place the story within the Mormon culture.

The film takes place in contemporary Provo, Utah, a city famous for the Mormon Brigham Young University (BYU). This first glimpses of this setting foreshadow the movie's reflection on the young (American) Mormon subculture on campus, including certain stereotypes of the age group, both Mormon and American. Overall criticism of the stereotypical superficiality of American young people, especially women, is perhaps best captured through the figure of Darcy, who is a rich, cultured, but somewhat stiff and snobbish British publisher visiting with his friend, Bingley. While his shortcomings are also dealt with through humor, Darcy is educated and values intelligence, loyalty, and a kind heart above all. In many ways, he is similar to Elizabeth Bennet, except that she mainly keeps her observations to herself, perhaps showing more tolerance and understanding than Darcy manages. She is a graduate student at BYU as well as an up-and-coming writer who, although 26, is not worried about being single.

Elizabeth lives with four housemates – replacing the sisters in the original novel – who all represent certain features of young female Mormon stereotypes, particularly on the BYU campus. This is a unique environment described so aptly by Taber as a marketplace where returned missionaries and female students – both driven by their desire as much as by Church expectations and family pressure to marry – are able to meet and find their life partner. A graduate from BYU recalls her experience there in an interview as follows: "BYU has a large number of returned missionaries who are bluntly shopping for a wife. I felt like a piece of merchandise instead of a human being" (Taber 333).

Elizabeth's landlady, Lydia, represents the woman who hears the call and understands the need to marry, so she is openly out on a hubbie hunt. Her apparent goal in life – marriage – is already implied in the introduction, which is also a general comment on the Mormon culture: "This is Lydia, our landlady. Actually, she made her parents buy the house to make her seem domestic. Apparently, guys like that." However, her domesticity seems to stop there, as she is only concerned about her appearance, knowing the power of the first impression. Still, she educates herself on the subject of hubbie hunting by reading the most popular book in the campus bookstore, *The Pink Bible: How to Bring your Man to his Knees* – which, as she observes at one point on the way to church, contains everything she needs to know in life. However, she never really attracts anyone serious because she is too superficial, vein, and unthinking – thus eloping to Las Vegas in the end with none other than the swindler Wickham, only to be rescued from marriage by her friends in the last minute.

Lydia's keen insistence on finding a proper, preferably wealthy husband – a topic she raises constantly in reference to Bingley, for example – even brings her into an unseemly competition with her other housemate, Jane. Upon arriving at the party she attends in the hopes of meeting and enthralling Bingley, she surveys the guests with her binoculars to find that Jane is dancing with him. She instantly calls out "Vulture!" and, determined to separate them, orders her sister, Kitty, to cut the electrical wiring to the loudspeakers. Jane also acts in a similar vein when she calls Lydia a "little tramp" for staying at Bingley's home the night of the party due to a hurt wrist. The movie humorously depicts the catty conflict in which certain young women may engage to capture Mr. Right.

On the other hand, Elizabeth's other housemate, Mary, exemplifies the good, traditional young Mormon woman: modest and obedient, kind but perhaps a bit too awkward, she exhibits a devotion to the Scriptures and Church literature that dictate her daily life. She lives and breathes LDS thought and Victorian values of proper womanhood. For example, she appears at Bingley's party in plain, old-fashioned clothes, carrying her embroidery kit with her, with her family tree as the pattern on the quilting cloth. She is enthralled by Collins' comment on the Pioneer Track – a reference to the historical struggles of Mormon settlers' crossing the North American continent to reach Mormon territory – and responds by enthusiastically telling the story of an aunt many generations removed, who had to sleep "inside a buffalo" to keep warm as she was crossing the trail. Mary's blind faith leads her into quite ridiculous but also piteous situations, such as when she picks up the Mormon magazine *Ensign* Collins has left behind and interprets the words "A virtuous woman never hides her light under a bushel" as a divine calling, prompting her to climb on stage and sing "My Bonnie" in a false voice and childish vein. Naturally, her fate is to fall for Collins, with whom she finds eternal love by the end of the movie, and they fittingly spend their honeymoon "on a Pioneer Track enactment."

In contrast to the hubbie hunter Lydia and the good Mormon girl Mary, the smart, talented, hard-working, independent-minded, and career-oriented figure of Elizabeth represents the modern Mormon woman – and the feminist challenge for Mormonism. As she states at the beginning of the movie: "It is a truth universally acknowledged that a girl of a certain age and in a certain situation in life must be in want of a husband. I guess I was in that situation and, according to my mother, I've passed that age quite some time ago." Still, she was, as Wickham put it, "the only girl not in the hunt," which made her so special – and at once unattainable – in his eyes. Her insistence on her superior judgment, her Bridget Jones-ian collapse when she turns out to be wrong, and her subsequent self-destructive escape into the world of junk food, overnight TV, and ever-accumulating trash all demonstrate her vulnerability along with her strong sense of character and conscience.

All three women have their male stereotypical parallels in the movie. Lydia's counterpart is her almost husband, Wickham, who does not even go to church any more, let alone observe the tenets of the faith. He is a Jack Mormon, who continues socializing with his old friends, including Elizabeth, who finds him amusing, but resents his "octopus hands" which he fails to keep to himself, his bigotry, and his exclusive interest in matters of the flesh. His opposite and current rival is Elizabeth's match, Darcy, who rebels by not wanting a boring, average wife, but a smart, exciting, unique person with whom to enjoy a happy married life. However, his somewhat exceptional expectations do not stand out in this basically patriarchal social milieu, and thus he appears on the screen as not particularly unusual, and thus a lesser target of humor than Elizabeth. His funny moments only reflect his own awkwardness and puzzlement over how he feels about her, for example, when he asks Elizabeth out in the bookstore; otherwise, his behavior is immaculate and rational.

The most humorous figure, however, is Mary's counterpart, Collins, the stereotype of the overtly proper, but goofy and awkward returned missionary. He is ready to make the appropriate next step in life in keeping with the expectations of the Church: to marry, as he imagined, "an old-fashioned girl", as he put it when proposing to Elizabeth. Chan offers an excellent characterization of his figure, but some specifically Mormon features must be pointed out here. One is his exaggerated conservatism and formality, from his appearance, such as his hairstyle, facial expressions, and manner of dress, to his language and choice of conversational topics, such as considering the Pioneer Track a fashionable topic because

Church News wrote about it, or admiring *Ensign* for containing "so many treasures". Such behavior may capture the attention of someone like Mary, but definitely not Elizabeth – which he fails to notice in his overt sense of self-certainty.

A scene in which he proposes to Elizabeth shows his conflated sense of patriarchy, through his initial incredulous response to Elizabeth's lack of enthusiasm at his proposal, and, as he gradually comes to accept her rejection, through his changed approach to Elizabeth, as signified by the names he uses for her, from Miss Bennet through Elizabeth to Missy. As a last resort, he even brings in his unquestionable patriarchal position as conveyor of God's will as he declares in a commanding voice: "Elizabeth, we've been commanded to multiply and replenish the Earth!", but the loud laughter of her housemates from the other room upsets anesmortifies him. He is deeply hurt and expresses his frustration at a church sacrament meeting as he describes a "worthy" man as a protector and provider for a woman, who should accept him in return and be a good wife, "drop out of school and stay at home as she is supposed to do." In her frustration, Elizabeth imagines throwing her *Book of Mormon* at him, signifying not only her disapproval of him, but also of his (and the Church's) idea that this is how marriage should be.

CONCLUSION

The numerous comical scenes in the movie all focus on the various stereotypes that capture certain human shortcomings found among Mormon youth, but never address tenets of the faith. These scenes seem to reflect what an LDS missionary said to us in an interview about his fellow Mormons: "Men are not perfect. Only God is." This movie also seems to reflect what Wilson concludes about LDS jokes: "contrary to the expectations of many, humor growing out of the Mormon experience will not always reveal a united people, sharing a common identity and viewing the world through similar eyes" (Wilson 9). The growing plurality among members of the LDS Church allows for a diversity of views, and thus viewers, of the movie. Cox argues that "a mature religious sense should include a good sense of humor" (quoted in Morreall 231). I trust that this movie, like other Mollywood comedies, signifies that Mormonism, as the Saints know it, has come of age, implying an understanding that self-reflective humor should not be considered as a form of attack and possible subversion of their faith and community. Hopefully, they are no longer the "estranged bedfellows" (Capps 413) they once used to be.

REFERENCES:

Annus, Irén. "Trans-Culturing Jane Austen: The Mollywood Adaptation of Pride and Prejudice." *Americana* 8.1 (2012). Web. 10 Sep. 2015. http://americanaejournal.hu/vol8no1/annus.

Austin, Michael. "The Function of Mormon Literary Criticism at the Present Time." *Dialogue* 28.4 (Winter 1994): 131-144. Web. 25 Sep. 2015. http://mldb.byu.edu/austin01.htm.

Baker, Margaret. "Humor." *Encyclopedia of Mormonism*. Vol. 2. MacMillan, 1992. Web. 26 Sep. 2015. http://www.lightplanet.com/mormons/humor/humor.html.

Black, Andrew (dir.). *Pride and Prejudice*. Written by Anne K. Black, Jason Faller and Katherine Swigart. Bestboy Productions/Excel Entertainment, 2003. Film.

Cannon, Ann Edwards. "And Now for a Little Mormon Humor." *Sunstone* 93 (Dec 1993): 16-21. Web. 2 Sep. 2015. https://www.sunstonemagazine.com/wp-content/uploads/sbi/articles/093-17-21.pdf.

Capps, Donald. "Religion and Humor: Estranged Bedfellows." *Pastoral Psychology* 54.5 (2006): 413-38. Print.

Chan, Mary M. "Mr. Collins on Screen: Jane Austen's Legacy of the Ridiculous." *Persuasions On-Line* 29.1 (2008). Web. 11 Apr. 2014. http://www.jasna.org/persuasions/on-line/vol29no1/chan.html.

Davies, Christie. "Introduction." In: *Jokes and their Relation to Society*. Ed. Christie Davies. Berlin: de Gruyter, 1998: 1-10. Print.

Davies, Christie. "The Protestant Ethic and the Comic Spirit of Capitalism." In: *Jokes and their Relation to Society*. Ed. Christie Davies. Berlin: de Gruyter, 1998: 43-62. Print.

LDS Filmography Pages. Web. 10 Sep. 2015. http://www.ldsfilm.com/.

Le Goff, Jacques. "Laughter in the Middle Ages." In: *A Cultural History of Humour: From Antiquity to the Present Day.* Eds. Jan Bremmer and Herman Roodenburg. Cambridge: Polity, 1977: 40-54. Print.

Morreall, John. "Philosophy and Religion." In: *The Primer of Humor Research.* Ed. Victor Ruskin. Berlin: Walter de Gruyter, 2008: 211-42. Print.

Norrick, Neal. "A Frame-Theoretical Analysis of Verbal Humor: Bisociation as Schemata Conflict." *Semiotica* 60.3-4 (1986): 225-245. Print.

Russell, Heddendorf. *From Faith to Fun: The Secularisation of Humour.* Cambridge: Luttenworth, 2009. Print.

Saroglou, Vassilis. "Religion and Sense of Humor: An a Priori Incompatibility? Theoretical Considerations from a Psychological Perspective." *Humor* 15.2 (2002): 191-214. Web. 12 Sep. 2015. http://www.ucllouvain.be/cps/ucl/doc/psyreli/documents/2002.Humor15.2.pdf.

Taber, Susan. *Mormon Lives: A Year in the Elkton Ward.* Urbana: University of Illinous Press, 1993. Print.

Tóth, Zsófia Anna. "Jane Austen Reloaded." *HUSSE10 – LitCult: Proceedings of the HUSSE 10 Conference.* Eds. Kinga Földváry, Zsolt Almási and Veronika Schandl. Debrecen: Hungarian Society for the Study of English, 2011: 302-310. Web. 11 Sep. 2015. http://mek.niif.hu/10100/10171/10171.pdf#page=313.

Wells, Juliette. "Jane Austen in Mollywood: Mainstreaming Mormonism in Andrew Black's *Pride and Prejudice.*" *Peculiar Portrayals: Mormons on Page, Stage, and Screen.* Eds. Mark T. Decker and Michael Austin. Logan, UT: Utah State University, 2010: 163-182. Print.

Wilson, William. "The Seriousness of Mormon Humor." *Sunstone* 45 (Jan. 1985): 6-13. Web. 26 Sep. 2015. https://www.sunstonemagazine.com/wp-content/uploads/sbi/articles/045-06-13.pdf.

Orsolya Anna Sudár

Memory Forgotten: the Importance of Narrative in Collective Memory Through Two Case Studies[1]

Introduction

In urban contexts, an inhabitant of a city is used to a constant siege of a multitude of narratives when it comes to places of memory. Our receptivity to narrative is a heritage acquired from modern urbanism itself and is a key to the formation of modern urban identity (Crinson xiv). The city of Sarajevo, for instance, presents us with multiple layers of narrative: that of the Turkish Empire, the Austrian destruction, and of course, the Bosnian War. The bullet holes and traces of grenades are open wounds on the city skin, but most importantly, they are living memorials.

Urban theory mainly agrees that places of memory, and what Pierre Nora calls *lieux de mémoire*, are demarked, physical sites where remembering is designed to take place (Nora 12). However, there are several narratives in memory and history with no spatial manifestation; as well as existing memorials that absorb wavering narratives. This paper is to discuss two instances in collective memory where neither spatiality nor

---

[1] This is a revised version of my paper entitled "Fingers of Impermanence: Expectations of urban disaster in and of the turn-of-century New York" to be published in the HJEAS journal in 2016.

narration is stable and firm: the Triangle Shirtwaist Factory fire of 1911 and the bombing of Wall Street of 1920.

SPATIALITY AND MEMORY

Juhani Pallasmaa, Finnish architect and theorist, claims in *Eyes of the Skin*: "We keep constructing an immense city of evocation and remembrance, and all the cities we have visited are precincts in the metropolis of the mind" (Pallasmaa 74). While the metaphor Pallasmaa uses ("Cities are human minds") stands at the basis of urban theory (de Certeau, Crinson, Young, Huyssen etc.), one must also notice the problem it raises regarding memory. This universal city of singular memories must be the place of continuity of memory, meaning that singular memories must fit into the greater collective of the universal "mind." The places of commemoration must be sanctuaries of memory, as Pierre Nora writes: "They mark the rituals of society without the ritual; integral particularities in a society that levels particularity; signs of distinction and of group membership in a society that tends to recognize individuals only as identical and equal" (Nora 12).

This means that memory in the urban context relies heavily on the physical manifestation of collective remembering; it is necessary that memory is substantiated into a memorial through which the individual is able to relate to the past and the present while also placing him or herself in the collective narrative. As in Mark Crinson's introduction to *Urban Memory*, in the traditional city memorials have the utopian function to connect individuals with the memories of their collective; in which system the city becomes its own living memorial (Crinson xvi). The monumentalist trend of the 19th century emerges from this very desire to found urban identity on a harmonious and reflective relationship with the past, where the monument is an apparatus of collective self-identification.

Baudelaire, Proust, Ruskin and Walter Benjamin were among the opponents to this trend; they agreed that architecture *per se* is a place of commemoration. For Benjamin, the building by the nature of time encompasses memory, thus it is a site of memory without the necessity of being a memorial. For Proust, memory is involuntary and is not necessarily consonant with collective narratives, but it is rather an internal and personal moment that is triggered by traces of personal importance. For Ruskin and Benjamin, a monument does not indicate a direct relation with past events but distances the individual from personal narratives through the reinforcement of collective ones.

The paradoxical outcome of this, the so called "crisis of memory" (Crinson xv), is a loss of memory: some memories enter collective memory in lieu of, and not besides, others. This results in collective amnesia taking place alongside the erection of memorials (Crinson xvi).

However, we can observe that in some cases forgotten memories come to the foreground unexpectedly, and/or when triggered by newer events. Allow me to apply Freud's theory of repressed traumas to the recurrence of buried collective memories. The recurrence of traumatic and repressed memories, according to Freud, may take place in dreams, moments of fear, and sometimes, in fantasies (Freud). In these unconscious re/actions (both action and re-action) the original traumatic event is continuously relived and reimagined: the individual ever positions him/herself within the traumatic situation; acting out what Freud calls the "compulsion to repeat" (Freud 205). Repetition, thus, functions here as a form of quotation, where in between the quotation marks an image is to occur.

This image and the nature of this very image stands at the heart of this paper: the visual memory, serving as a connection to the past even when buried and unremembered. In the network of citations, the image is a document that is taken to be objective and truthful to its subject, whatever its nature: mental or photographic. On photographic images, Roland Barthes argues that in the context of illustration, the image elucidates the text as well as it realizes it (Barthes 25). In other words, the juxtaposition of text and image does not invite a hierarchical relationship where the image illustrates text but the other way around: the primary text is the image and the secondary is the text itself. Accordingly, it is via the photograph that both texts, written and photographic, in our cultural reading become "analogons" of reality. How do these texts change the way memories are handled?

Re/presentation and narration

The fire that broke out in the Triangle Shirtwaist Factory on March 25, 1911, is one of the most vividly remembered tragedies of the first decade of the 20th century. It has become a symbol of workers' rights, women's rights, and the fight against the exploitation of immigrants in the United States. A factory, strikingly similar to the Triangle, is the setting of Michael Cunningham's ghost story *In the Machine*. The fire was also one of the first major incidents in New York where photography served as a journalistic apparatus. On March 26, the New York Times published a commemorative article with a photograph: we see three police officers gazing at a building in paralyzed terror, with twisted bodies of women at their feet. However, as Tina Margolis argues in her essay, this photo may be inauthentic to the event, for the fall of the girls in the photograph and the gaze of the officers (as well as their physical positions) are logistically impossible. Margolis also builds on a research that showed there was no neighboring building to the factory ever having columns at its foot, serving as a monumental mise-en-scène to the published photo.

The presumption, therefore, is that the most commonly referenced photo of the fire is in fact a set image: a dramatized scene of real events. If the photograph is read as an illustration and not a preliminary text, the tragic scene of the fire instantly becomes an aestheticized image: one in which the objects of connotation are preordained, constructed, and condensed in a way that they would reinforce the (direct or indirect) memory of the original scene. The image thus becomes a piece of art and an artifact of the collective processing of trauma. Barthes claims that pose itself is a connotative procedure in which the receiver of the image disregards the pose *per se*, but instead reads the posed image on the denotative level (Barthes 22). Therefore, it is the iconographic setting that allows the fire-photograph to be instantly read as pure denotation, something that represents unscripted action. It is perhaps precisely the scriptedness of this very photograph that makes it readable within the confines of reality. While the original scene and photographs taken at the fire are by definition unscripted, their reading tends to remain in the terrains of the denotative: the pure description which does not leave room for subjective interpretation and/or personal decoding of message. While representation and iconicization lift the traumatic scene to the level of the sacred (thus, as a text, it becomes sacred), descriptive narration refuses to (and cannot) purify given realities. Consequently, the commemoration of the Triangle Fire is most accurate through the fictionalization thereof: the primary text as an emblematic image remains in the terrains of fiction.

While the staged, posed, choreographed photograph analyzed here fails to be an analogon of reality, furthermore fails to realize the "illustrating" text or to serve as hypotext in the network of citations of memories, it does nevertheless function as a sanctuary of traumatic memory. It is the fictive narrative inscribed into the photo that makes it citable and thus sacred; the photograph gives us the sense that it is truer than truth itself, as it also refuses the "murderous power of images" as Baudrillard calls it, the "murderers of the real, murderers of their own model, as the Byzantine icons could be those of divine identity" (Baudrillard a 5). The Asch building, now called Brown Building, is part of the New York University campus with a rather small plaque on the corner of Washington Place and Green Street. While the images of the fire entered collective memory and circulate in it continually, a separate memorial site remains absent from the city of New York. As in Cunningham's novel, the fire prevails as an indirect memory, a point of reference and an allegory; and it is in this state of indirectness that we can find its proper site of memory.[2]

MISSING DOCUMENTS: UNNAMABLE MEMORY

While in the case of the Triangle *lieu de mémoire* seems to claim space in fictitious images of memory, in many cases of collective tragedy we cannot speak of such commemorative reference points. My other case study, the 1920 bombing of Wall Street, is such an example. Despite the terror attack being highly symbolic in its location and timing, it remains on

---

[2] A thorough analysis is to be found in László Munteán's dissertation-chapter titled "The Outer Edge of Memory: Literary Representations" in the yet unpublished disseration Munteán.

the periphery of collective remembering when it comes to terror attacks: attacks on distinctively American principles and the American sentiment in general. The attack took place at the corner of Wall and Broad, in front of J. P. Morgan & Company, and the Stock Exchange buildings; at the angles of this triad stand the foundations of the United States: freedom, free-market, and capitalism. It could have been, and was intended to be, similar to what Baudrillard calls the "symbolic collapse" of the World Trade Center Towers, where the primary target was the symbol itself (48).

One reason for the attack's absence from collective memory might be the complete absence of press coverage: only two photos are to be found in connection with the bombing, both showing the scene at a distance and without care for detail. This lack of detail is what allows for a lack of symbolism in visual memory – something that is, according to Baudrillard, crucial for the victory of terrorism (Baudrillard b 31). This event, in fact, refuses to be an event of terror for it fails to induce actual fear (*terreur*).[3] A refusal of *terreur* flashes back in the photographs of the attack: descriptive and failing to capture the narrative of fear itself. In these images the personalization of trauma observed in the case of the Triangle Fire (and 9/11) does not occur. As Baudrillard puts it: "The image consumes the event in the sense that it absorbs it and offers it for consumption" (Baudrillard b 30). This consumption does not occur in the case of the 1920 bombing.

As the attack does not become a marked event in collective visual memory (in lack of documentation), it fails to become a name, as in Derrida's understanding, too. September 11, as a name, according to Derrida, is in itself a citation of memories: it is *fait date* (marks an event) because it is metonymical of collectively and personally significant details that are unparalleled in (personal and collective) memory; and since it is, in lack of precedent of any form, unidentifiable and unrecognizable, it must be placed within the "*supposedly* universal calendar" as a singular and universal event (Borradori 87). As Derrida argues, the fait date naming of event is a form of Freudian repetition, also an acting out of "the compulsion

---

[3] It was also the intention of New York magnates to have as few reports as possible so that stock institutions could reopen (Gage).

to repeat" the traumatic event (Borradori 89). Accepting that the act of naming September 11 "9/11," "September 11", putting it between quotation marks, is an act of endless reiteration, one may wonder according to what rules are some events placed in the universal calendar and some not. The 1920 bombing, though the most significant terror attack in the US of its time, is not *fait date*, did not enter the calendar and, consequently, did not become subject of endless reiteration. The 1920 bombing, taking place on September 16 did not become *fait-date*.

Nevertheless, the terror attack of 1920 does become subject of debate and historical research after 2001. It seems as if the events of 9/11 had triggered some necessity to rediscover and remember other instances of terror and trauma. It was historian Beverly Gage who first published a separate volume on the bombing in 2008; Gage gives us a clear image, however, as to what lead to the explosion of Wall Street. While 9/16 is an inexistent name, the bombing does have a linking narrative to 9/11: the collective expectation of disaster, the fantasies of an ultimate attack on shared values that posteriorly circulate in the collective unconscious. In relation to 9/11, Baudrillard himself claims "the fact that we have dreamt of this event, that everyone without exception had dreamt of it – because no one can avoid dreaming of the destruction of any power that has become hegemonic to this degree – is unacceptable to the Western moral conscience" (Baudrillard a 5). Also, after the 1920 bombing, the *Washington Post* wrote: "What we have expected has happened, New York has been blown up" (in Gage 125). In this network of posterior recognition, signs of looming disaster gain meaning, as in Andreas Huyssen's essay "Twin Memories: Afterimages of 9/11." Huyssen calls the destruction of the Buddhas of Bamiyan by the Taliban a prologue of 9/11, pointing out the striking similarities between the symbolism of the two monuments and their violent destruction (Huyssen 159). Both were twin-monuments and both remained an empty space, representing the vast absence thereof. It can be claimed therefore that the destructive symbolism behind both the attack on the Buddhas of Bamiyan and the Twins were based on the concept of absence; however, this does not convincingly make the dynamiting of the Buddhas a "prologue" to the destruction of the Towers carried out in *jihad*. Had it been a prologue, and not a similarly symbolic act of violence, 9/11 would not have demanded the life of so many: we must always distinguish between mere iconoclasm and iconoclasm that also holds human death at its aim.

CONCLUSION

"The Wall Street bombing", "the 1920 bombing", "the attack of 1920" the names to call the terror attack on Wall Street in 1920, cannot re/present the actual event: something that we think is the terror attack of 1920. The name does not fit because it is "no name," it is anonymous, in the sense that it can bear no name. This is, of course, a linguistic problem, but it is also that of memory. How can we remember something that bears no name; how can we build a monument for something we cannot name?

The case studies analyzed here are both, in some way, un- or mis-remembered: the memory of the Triangle fire is iconicized by fictional narratives and accordingly, enters collective memory as not an event in the Heideggerian sense but a scene to be visually absorbed, which is also the optical memory of the state of falling and fire. In the case of the bombing, the only narrative that circles around the relatively small memory of the event is expectation itself, a link that ties September 16 to "September 11" in an impossible competition for recognition. The above raised question stands at the heart of this paper for the cases studied here present to us elements of history that have been marginalized despite their objective historical significance; the challenge they present lies not in the process of remembering but in that of "unforgetting": an imagined and idealized process that is built around the vast absence of memory and recognizes forgetting as an elemental part of remembering itself.

REFERENCES:

Barthes, Roland. "The Photographic Message." In: Idem, *Image-Music-Text*. London: Macmillan, 1978: 15-32. Print.

Baudrillard, Jean a. *Simulacra and Simulation*. Ann Arbor: University of Michigan press, 1994.

— b. *The Spirit of Terrorism and Other Essays*. London & NY Verso, 2003. Print.

Borradori, Giovanna. *Philosophy in a Time of Terror: Dialogues with Jurgen Habermas and Jacques Derrida*. Chicago: University of Chicago Press, 2003. Print.

Crinson, Mark. "Urban Memory: an Introduction." In: Idem, *Urban Memory: History and Amnesia in the Modern City* (2005): xi-xx.

Cunningham, Michael. *Specimen Days: A Novel*. London: Macmillan, 2007. Print.

Freud, Sigmund. *Beyond the Pleasure Principle*. Broadview Press, 2011. Reprint.

Gage, Beverly. *The Day Wall Street Exploded: A Story of America in its First Age of Terror*. Oxford: Oxford University Press, 2008. Print.

Huyssen, Andreas. "Twin Memories: Afterimages of 9/11." *Present Pasts: Urban Palimpsests and the Politics of Memory*. Stanford: Stanford University Press, 2003: 158-177. Print.

Margolis, Tina, Karen Keller and Julie Rones. "Constructed Memory and the Paradox of Empathy: Reconsidering an Image of the Triangle Fire." *Afterimage* 39.1/2 (2011): 25-28. *Academic Search Complete*. Web. 14 Apr. 2014.

Munteán, László. "Topographies of Trauma: Constellations of the Corporeal and the Architectural in Representations of 9/11." Diss. Eötvös Loránd U, Department of Humanities, Doctoral School of Literary Studies, American Studies, 2011. Print. Publication in progress.

Nora, Pierre. "Between Memory and History: Les Lieux de Mémoire." *Representations* 26 (1989): 7-29. Print.

Pallasmaa, Juhani. *The Eyes of the Skin: Architecture and the Senses*. John Wiley & Sons, 2012. Print.

"Photos & Illustrations." *Remembering the 1911 Triangle Factory Fire*. Cornell University, n.d. Web. 14 Jan. 2014.

"The Wall Street Explosion." *The New York Times*.17 Sep. 1920: n. pag. *New York Times Archive*. Web. 2 Mar. 2014.

IVAN LACKO

(Re)dramatizing, (Re)framing and (Re)writing History in Suzan-Lori Parks' *The America Play*

Suzan-Lori Parks' *The America Play* has given a new meaning to the significance of absence as a creative incentive to re-assess the role of historical and political circumstances in the social development in the United States. The 'hole' she positions in the center of her endeavor is representative of the void in the African American construction of identity brought about by negating the dominant, 'white' influence in the making and interpretation of history. In a typically playful and multifaceted manner, Parks creates a dramatic world that makes use of holes, absences and voids to help (re)claim the cultural identity of black Americans and offers audiences a broader context in which historical constants are rewritten through entirely new prisms of cultural heritage.

My objective in this paper is to show that the metaphorical concept of absence to create presence and content helps Parks build a musical structure allowing her to review, repeat and revise historical events and extend them by new symbols and meanings. I believe that the inquiry I aim to conduct is valid not only in the context of the academic study of American cultural and political issues, but also as part of the scrutiny of how the specifically American experience with race, ethnicity, identity and understanding of history is relevant for the Central European historical and cultural context. The central theme in Suzan-Lori Parks' seminal play reflects the significance of 'holes' or 'absence' in the social-political development and history of post-communist countries. I would like to underscore the importance of recognizing, and subsequently divulging, the mechanics of framing a country's historical and cultural awareness. In terms of the capability to uncover the processes that underlie such framing, a society (or its smaller communities) becomes able to produce instruments that ultimately unframe (or reframe) its history, culture and politics.

The America Play opens with the following stage instructions: "A great hole. In the middle of nowhere. The hole is an exact replica of the Great Hole of History" (Parks d 159). This not only establishes Parks' extremely fragmented narrative, but also communicates her resolve to use the space of this hole for a search and inquiry. For Parks, this becomes an opportunity to use the theatrical world to produce a new (or alternate) history because, in her own words, "so much of African-American history has been unrecorded, dismembered, washed out" (Parks c 4). Parks sees her role as an artist who can now "locate the ancestral burial ground, dig for bones, find bones, hear the bones sing, write it down" (Parks c 4). The process of digging and writing things down – alongside the macabre image of singing bones – then becomes an instrument of history-making and offers a chance to start from scratch, or indeed, from an empty hole. Unlike regular historians, who write history in sequence and draw on the past events that have already been framed by previous historians, researchers or even politicians, Parks' creative 'big bang' sets in motion all kinds of historical stories and makes it possible to introduce a variety of re-enactments. Mehdi Ghasemi, for example, claims that "[r]ewriting historical events with new significations admittedly helps Parks both to challenge and change readers'/audiences' perceptions of American history as the only valid, valuable and voiced version of history and to redefine and refine their perceptions of African American history" (Ghasemi 133), subscribing to the notion that there might as well be "a semantic relationship between the hole of History and the need to revise such history to make it whole" (Bernard 688).

To be able to perform a revision of history, Parks introduces her main character, the Foundling Father, as Abraham Lincoln, also known as the

Lesser Known. He is African American and bears a striking resemblance to America's famous president, referenced to in the play as the Great Man. This challenges the audience's conventional views of Lincoln. Parks combines the words 'foundling' and 'father' to confront our common understanding of the words, particularly because we immediately make the association with 'the founding fathers'. The Lesser Known, a gravedigger, is then involved in a series of scenes that never form a linear narrative and are regularly replayed and reviewed using the approach Parks calls "Rep&Rev", or "Repetition and Revision". Echoing the composition and performance of music, particularly jazz, "Rep&Rev" becomes a tool allowing Parks to move the story forward through a structure of rhythmically interconnected elements, putting them together in a kind of "incremental refrain" (Parks b 9). In this context, the author's decision to repeat, revise and rewrite unmistakably draws on Henry Louis Gates's concept of Signifyin(g), according to which there should always be "formal revision and an intertextual relation" (Gates 51), including not just a structural review, but also a revision of language through which a "historically nameless community of remarkably self-conscious speakers of English defined their ontological status as one of profound difference vis-a-vis the rest of society" and delineated themselves by means of what Gates refers to as "a (re)naming ritual" that leads to self-signification (Gates 47).

The mere fact that such an iconic personality as Abraham Lincoln becomes an instrument of experimental theatre makes *The America Play* an exceptional undertaking. As Deborah R. Geis suggests, Parks not only "[rewrites iconic characters] through the prism of African American cultural history" (Geis 98), but does so in a way that blurs the lines between the past and present, between words and silence, and between presentational theater and metatheater.[1] The deliberate transgression of conventional form

---

[1] This approach is typical of Parks and can be traced also in her other works, most notably in *Topdog/Underdog* which is a dramatic account of the lives of two brothers, Lincoln and Booth, both African American and struggling with the economic, racial and cultural consequences of their uprbringing. Similarly, Parks' rewrite of classic American literature in *Fucking A* and *In the Blood* in which she introduces characters named Hester La Negrita and Hester Smith as offshoots of the famous character of Hester Prynne in Nathaniel Hawthorne's *The Scarlet Letter*.

then results in the need to employ different means of communication. The rewriting of history that Parks is intent on doing will eventually require a whole new set of signifiers. Joseph R. Roach posits that plays that go beyond traditional forms, including *The America Play*, will "seek other languages for their retelling – languages of image, of gesture, of sound, and especially of silence" (Roach 307). Silence becomes an integral part of the play's structure in the inherent historical void Parks tries to fill. For Parks, whose theatrical form is consciously musical, silence not only "creates a space and rhythm, designating something" (Suk and Neprašová 291) but also becomes what Lilijana Herakova and her co-researchers refer to as "a statement of belonging" made to the white majority concerning racial issues and "contributing to whiteness as a system of dominance in the United States" (Herakova 376). The following extract from *The America Play* demonstrates how Parks applies her musical Rep&Rev style to recapitulate the assassination by means of fast-forwarding a video recording of a theatrical scene as well as how silence, originally the result of shock and dismay, becomes selective silence that redefines a particular historical event (the assassination of Abraham Lincoln and its consequences):

> And now, the centerpiece of the evening!! *(Rest)* Uh Behm. The Death of Lincoln!: – The watching of the play, the laughter, the smiles of Lincoln and Mary Todd, the slipping of Booth into the presidential box unseen, the freeing of the slaves, the pulling of the trigger, the bullets piercing above the left ear, the bullets entrance into the great head, the bullets lodging behind the great right eye, the slumping of Lincoln, the leaping onto the stage of Booth, the screaming of Todd, the screaming of Todd, the screaming of Keene, the leaping onto the stage of Booth; the screaming of Todd, the screaming of Keene, the shouting of Booth "Thus to the tyrants!," the death of Lincoln! – And the silence of the nation. (Parks d 188)

The America Play successfully projects the complexity of the context in which both personal and political matters arise: this is mostly visible in the multiple-layered structure of the play itself and the construction and reconstruction of the identity of Parks' characters. The former element takes shape, for example, in the playwright's concept of time, as Katy Ryan suggests: "In Parks' dramaturgy, 'now and then' is not chronologically but spatially conceived; death is always present and has something to say. The Lesser Known tries to follow in the Great Man's footsteps 'that were of course *behind* him,' impossibly trying to *'catch up'* to the past" (Ryan 85). Echoing the last lines of *The Great Gatsby*, this is Parks' take on the nature of the American dream – a vast space full of holes that seem both desolate and devastating, yet are also filled with potential. The latter element revolves around the play's comprehensive structure and form. Parks underscores that for her, "form and content are interdependent" and that "[i]t's like this: I am an African-American woman – this is the form I take, my content predicates this form, and this form is inseparable from my content. No way could I be otherwise" (Parks b 8).

This might suggest that identity building is, somewhat paradoxically, both predetermined and not determinable. At any rate, identity is formed in a process that excludes a person's free will, or, as Lucia Otrísalová proposes, "we do not have a free choice when constructing an identity to present to others, but we negotiate it with others in our culture and society" (Otrísalová 182). This negotiation often rests on the ability to amalgamate the personal and political – something Parks successfully achieves, corroborating Tony Kushner's opinion that in socially engaged theater, "[e]verything is personal; everything is political" (Kushner 22). Consequently, any discussion about political theater in relation to Suzan-Lori Parks' *The America Play* leads to another claim by Kushner, namely, that in drama or performance, the most intriguing issues are the unfathomable ones, in other words, problems "which no political theory or belief in human agency can address, which lie beyond politics, beyond history, in the realm of destiny, tragedy, and myth" (Kushner 21). For Parks, this is where her drama starts, giving way to an approach that challenges all of the above mentioned elements, especially myth. Parks' employment of 'holes' and 'bones' reiterates Joe Kelleher's illustrious suggestion that the function of "both politics and theatre [lies in] the very activities of showing and saying through which some are made visible who would otherwise have 'no business' being seen" (Kelleher 68). This is exactly what Parks unframes and reframes in *The America Play* – the invisibility of African American history and the subsequent conspicuousness of its individual protagonists even in 'white' history.

In her short essay *An Equation for Black People Onstage*, Parks explains how the creative approach is driven by her desire to escape the demarcation of 'black' drama merely as an opposition to 'white' drama and posits that black drama should go beyond just presenting the black as oppressed. The equation then goes as follows:

> black people + x = new dramatic conflict (new territory) where x is the realm of situations showing African-Americans in states other than the Oppressed by/Obsessed with "Whitey" state; where the white when present is not the oppressor, and where audiences are encouraged to see and understand and discuss these dramas in terms other than that same old shit. (Parks a 19-20)

This playful mathematical definition of the source of material for dramatic performance endows *The America Play* with a dimension within which Parks can experiment with multiple meanings and ambiguity – features that help her offer a revision of history and challenge it at the same time. It is not viable to use the play's multi-layered arrangement to attempt to arrive at a straightforward interpretation of any single scene which, in turn, makes it "difficult, or even impossible, to think about this play in traditional literary and dramatic terms" (Haike 10).

Another element that inhibits a straightforward interpretation of Parks' play is its apparent metatheatrical nature. The playwright's claim at rewriting history relies on the performers and the staging to produce a piece (or rather, event) that draws on its being already 'staged' in the same sense in which Lionel Abel delineated metatheater:

> What dramatized [such events] originally? Myth, legend, past literature, they themselves. They represent to the playwright the effect of dramatic imagination before he has begun to exercise his own; on the other hand, unlike figures in tragedy, they are aware of their own theatricality. Now, from a certain point of view, only that life which has acknowledged its inherent theatricality can be made interesting on the stage. (Abel 135).

But in Parks' case, this 'inherent theatricality' is to be found in the very series of historical events she is bent on (re)dramatizing, (re)framing and (re)writing. In many respects, Parks fumbles with the dramatic tools that were once used to frame African-American history in a haphazard and seemingly irrational manner by deconstructing and undermining the white formula used in the process of framing in the first place. She does not want to write "the text we are told to write" (Parks b 8) – instead, she escapes the dramatic linearity and attempts to offer a (re)production of history while constantly questioning and undermining the audience's sensitivity to it: "By claiming that the staging of an historical event makes it 'actually happen,' [Parks] thus creates a way to challenge our perception of reality and history" (Haike 5).

The America Play presents an undertaking that aims to deconstruct a system of structures that signify meaning in our perception of history with a focus on the African American experience of history and its representation and interpretation. This focus is applied specifically to the process of "digging and holes [which helps Parks establish] a new way of 'digging' the past to look at the world" (Geis 163). This process is performative and theatrical; it challenges the conventional awareness of history and its events, and provides an opportunity to fill the metaphorical hole with new meaning, symbolism and discourse. The play ends with a tableau of the deceased Abraham Lincoln lookalike who fills the grave – the great hole of history:

> [O]ur newest Wonder: One of thuh greats Hisself! Note: body sitting propped upright in our great Hole. Note the large mouth opened wide. Note the top hat and frock coat, just like the greats. Note the death wound: thuh great black hole – thuh great black hole in thuh great head. – And how this great head is bleedin. – Note: thuh last words. – And thuh last breaths. – And how thuh nation mourns – (Parks a 199)

At the same time, the performative character of the tableau itself is a deliberate reminder of both the necessity to review and revise historical events, and the possible ineffectiveness of such an endeavor. What remains, however, is the realization that the will and effort to challenge the construction of these events is always important.

References:

Abel, Lionel. *Tragedy and Metatheatre: Essays on Dramatic Form*. New York: Holmes & Meier, 2003. Print.

Bernard, Louise. "The Musicality of Language: Redefining History in Suzan-Lori Parks' The Death of the Last Black Man in the Whole Entire World." *African American Review* 31.4 (1997): 687-98. Print.

Gates, Henry L. *The Signifying Monkey: A Theory of Afro-American Literary Criticism*. New York: Oxford University Press, 1988. Print.

Geis, Deborah R. *Suzan-Lori Parks*. Ann Arbor: University of Michigan Press, 2008. Print.

Ghasemi, Mehdi. "History Plays As/Or Counterhistory Plays: A Study of Suzan-Lori Parks' Major Plays." *Marang: Journal of Language and Literature* 24 (2014): 123-35. Print.

Haike, Frank. "The Instability of Meaning in Suzan-Lori Parks' The American Play." *American Drama* 11.2 (2002): 4-20. Print.

Herakova, Lilijana et al. "Voicing Silence and Imagining Citizenship: Dialogues about Race and Whiteness in a "Postracial" Era." *Communication Studies* 62.4 (2011): 372-88. Print.

Kelleher, Joe. *Theatre & Politics*. Houndmills, Basingstoke, Hampshire [England], New York: Palgrave Macmillan, 2009. Print.

Kushner, Tony. "Notes about Political Theater." *The Kenyon Review* 19.3-4 (1997). Print.

Otrísalová, Lucia. "Naming and Identity in Lawrence Hill's Someone Knows My Name." In: *Identity in Intercultural Communication: Slovak Studies in English III*. Ed. Ada Böhmerová. Bratislava: ŠEVT, 2011: 182-89. Print.

Parks, Suzan-Lori a. "An Equation for Black People Onstage." In: Eadem. *The America Play, and Other Works*. 1st ed. New York: Theatre Communications Group, 1995: 19-22. Print.

— b. "From Elements of Style." In: Eadem. *The America Play, and Other Works*. 1st ed. New York: Theatre Communications Group, 1995: 6-18. Print.

—. "Possession." In: Eadem. *The America Play, and Other Works*. 1st ed. New York: Theatre Communications Group, 1995: 3-5. Print.

—. *The America Play, and Other Works*. 1st ed. New York: Theatre Communications Group, 1995: Print.

Roach, Joseph R. "The Great Hole of History: Liturgical Silence in Beckett, Osofisan, and Parks." *The South Atlantic Quarterly* 100.1 (2001): 307-17. Print.

Ryan, Katy. "'No Less Human': Making History in Suzan-Lori Parks' *The America Play.*" *Journal of Dramatic Theory and Criticism* 13.2 (1999): 81-94. Print.

Suk, Jan and Olga Neprašová. "The Phenomenon of Silence in the Post-dramatic Oeuvre of Forced Entertainment in Theory and Practice." In: *From Theory to Practice 2012: Proceedings of the Fourth International Conference on Anglophone Studies: September 5-6, 2012, Tomas Bata University in Zlín, Czech Republic.* Eds. Gregory J. Bell, Katarína Nemčoková and Bartosz Wójcik. Zlín: Univerzita Tomáše Bati ve Zlíně, 2013: 289-302. Print.

Abstracts

Radosław Rybkowski
Across the Atlantic. Why American Studies in Poland?
The paper explores the early foundations of American Studies in Poland. Such figures as Thaddeus Kosciuszko or Casimir Pulaski fought for American independence; during the times of partitions, many Poles migrated to the United States. This established natural ties between Poland and the United States, Polish and American culture and society. However, it was at the beginning of the 20th century that the first example of research in American Studies emerged. Professor Roman Dyboski set the grounds for the field of studies which is flourishing today. Some of his questions still remain valid, such as the topic of the roots and features of American civilization.

Prezentowany szkic ukazuje początki studiów amerykanistycznych w Polsce. Udział Polaków (np. Tadeusza Kościuszki czy Kazimierza Pułaskiego) w walce o niepodległość Stanów Zjednoczonych, liczne migracje z ziem polskich wytworzyły naturalne więzy pomiędzy obydwoma państwami, także w wymiarze kulturowym i społecznym. Niemniej jednak dopiero wiek XX przyniósł narodziny badań amerykanistycznych w Polsce. Prekursorem w tej dziedzinie był profesor Roman Dyboski, badający źródła cywilizacji amerykańskiej. Wiele ze stawianych przez niego pytań pozostaje aktualnych do dziś.

Réka M. Cristian

Mapping an Remapping America(s): Perspectives on Hungarian American Studies

This article surveys the development of American studies in Hungary by focusing on American studies as an institutionalized academic discipline and envisages the current practice of the field in the Hungarian university both in the regional and in the global context by concentrating on the cultural production, re-construction and re-evaluation of diverse issues, processes and concepts seen from the Hungarian perspective today. The development of American studies in Hungary has had similar paradigm shifts with the American field of study within various changing frameworks, starting from the myth and symbol school synthesis of literature and history to the strategies adopted by the New Americanists leading to the current post-national, transnational American studies. Nevertheless, American studies in Hungary has had its own idiosyncrasies as well, since American studies played a distinctive, subversive role within Hungarian higher education during the Cold War decades and was an important catalyzer in the production and interpretation of realities in the following years, when the country's higher education witnessed an emergence of American studies departments at various universities and colleges, alongside the proliferation of multiple printed and electronic books, journals and other publications related to the study of the US together with numerous conferences and research groups, the founding in 1992 of the Hungarian Association for American Studies (HAAS), which has been also member of the European Association for American Studies (EAAS) since 1994, and of the Center for Interamerican Studies at the University of Szeged, in 2015.

Tanulmányom a magyarországi amerikanisztika rövid történetét mutatja be a terület egyetemi intézményesedésének fontosabb mozzanatain keresztül. Kitérek a jelenlegi hazai módszerekre és megközelítésekre, kutatói csoportokra és konferenciákra, tanszékekre és publikációkra, amelyek a jelenlegi globális kontextusban lokális, illetve regionális meglátásokkal gazdagítják a területet. A magyar amerikanisztika fiatal tudományterület Magyarországon; a hidegháború végére az addig szubverzívnek számító terület, melynek különféle megközelítései léteztek ugyan az ország nagyobb egyetemein sikerrel intézményesedett több fontos tanszék és amerikanisztika program megalapításával, valamint a Amerikanisták Magyarországi Társaság (Hungarian Association for American Studies, HAAS), illetve később az Inter-Amerika Kutatóközpont létrejöttével.

Peter Rusiňák
From Hardware to Soft Skills – North American Area Studies in Slovakia. A View from Bratislavian Center for North American Studies Experience

American Studies, or, in Slovak, *Amerikanistika*, has traditionally been represented amongst academic subjects available to university students across various Slovak higher education institutions and their study programs. In fact, this slightly veiled title has been attracting the attention of numerous generations of students seeking their degree in a prospective discipline. Furthermore, and most importantly, Amerikanistika depicts the American dream – a bright future with a dream job, a work-life balance in the most prosperous countries in the world and many more benefits. Similar thoughts have been striking the minds of students interested in enrolling mainly in Faculties of Arts (Philosophy, Social Studies or Philology) in Slovakia. Unfortunately, they have been surprised by the fact that Amerikanistika no longer represents the bright future of a prospective career and that it is becoming increasingly difficult to stay competitive on the EU job market with a degree in American Studies from Slovak universities.

The author explains why American studies programs are not dead in the Slovak environment. He is convinced that they only need an upgrade in order to adapt to the needs of local and global markets and to provide a solid foundation for students whose demand to study the fascinating world of Amerikanistika has not decreased over time.

„Americké štúdiá", respektíve „Amerikanistika", boli tradične súčasťou akademickej ponuky pre budúcich vysokoškolských študentov viacerých slovenských univerzít a vzdelávacích inštitúcií. Tento jemne tajomný a všeobecný názov pútal pozornosť viacerých generácií študentov usilujúcich o vzdelanie v perspektívnej oblasti. Amerikanistika im vykresľovala ich americký sen – svetlú budúcnosť s vysnívanou prácou, rovnováhu medzi vlastným životom a prácou v elitárskych krajinách, ako aj ďalšie benefity. Tieto myšlienky vírili v hlavách slovenských študentov usilujúcich sa o prijatie hlavne na humanisticky zamerané fakulty (filozofia, sociálne štúdiá, filológia). Nanešťastie títo študenti zistili, že štúdium amerikanistiky už nejaký čas nezaručuje svetlú budúcnosť s perspektívnou kariérou a že je čím ďalej tým náročnejšie ostať konkurencieschopný na trhu práce s diplomom z amerických štúdií zo slovenských univerzít.

V tomto článku autor vysvetľuje, prečo programy amerických štúdií napriek tomu nie sú v slovenskom vysokoškolskom prostredí mŕtve. Je presvedčený, že potrebujú čerstvý upgrade, aby sa mohli adaptovať potrebám miestneho a globálneho trhu a poskytnúť plnohodnotný základ tým študentom, ktorých fascinujúci svet amerických štúdií stále láka. Tu začína príbeh CNAS...

Ewelina Gutowska-Kozielska
At War with Hillary. The Constitutive Rhetoric of the Republican Party
In this paper I focus on the constitutive function of the rhetoric of Rush Limbaugh, a representative of the Republican Party, which, like the majority of political parties or ideologies, is capable, in the rhetorical dimension, of existence only in opposition to/at war with something, that enemy being the vital ideograph of the organization. Thus, the very process of rhetorical creation of that enemy and the techniques of fighting against them are, in fact, fundamental for the constitutive rhetoric of the party. The enemy – here embodied by Hillary Clinton – is inseparably connected with the concept of power and dominance, the latter being the indispensable tool of the administration of mental control, which, in turn, creates possibilities of changing the existing reality or establishing an alternative one.

Niniejszy tekst jest próbą analizy konstytutywnej funkcji retoryki Rusha Limbaugha jako reprezentanta Partii Republikańskiej. Partia ta, podobnie jak inne tego typu organizacje bądź ideologie, w wymiarze retorycznym może istnieć wyłącznie w opozycji/stanie wojny przeciw *wrogowi* będącemu kluczowym ideografem organizacji. Proces retorycznego konstruowania owych wrogów i techniki używane, aby z nimi walczyć, stanowią podstawę konstytutywnej retoryki partii. Wróg – tu uosabiany przez Hillary Clinton – jest nieodłącznie związany z pojęciami władzy i dominacji niezbędnych dla zapewnienia kontroli mentalnej odbiorcy, co, z kolei, tworzy możliwość retorycznej rekonstrukcji istniejącej rzeczywistości bądź stworzenia rzeczywistości alternatywnej.

Jan Bečka, Maxim Kucer
The US Pivot to Asia: Historical Reflection, Current Situation and Perspectives for the Future

The article deals with the so-called American "pivot to Asia". Announced in 2011 by Hillary Clinton and Barack Obama, the "pivot" was seen as a major shift in the US foreign policy which, when implemented, would divert the main part of the US military, political and economic assets to Asia-Pacific. The justification behind this move was to improve the US image in Asia-Pacific, revive the relations with some of the long-standing American allies, and, tacitly, to check the growing assertiveness of the People's Republic of China. After almost four years since the "pivot" was announced, it is obvious that it is not a groundbreaking change. The United States has not abandoned Europe, as some have predicted, nor it has made Asia-Pacific its absolute, utmost priority. Yet, it has been able to achieve tangible results, both in improving its image and in becoming more active in the Asian multinational organizations and in the local geo-strategic and security framework. The Trans-Pacific Partnership, if finalized, would be a unique project in itself and could serve as a precedent for similar projects with Europe and other parts of the world.

Studie „The New American Pacific Century: The US "Pivot" to Asia, Its Implementation and Its Consequences" se zaměřuje americkou zahraniční politiku v oblasti Asie a Tichomoří během dvou prezidentských období Baracka Obamy. Právě Obamova administrativa oznámila v roce 2011 zásadní přehodnocení americké politické, vojenské a obchodní přítomnosti v Asii, která později vešla ve známost jako „pivot to Asia". Iniciativa byla snahou oživit vztahy s některými americkými spojenci, ujistit asijské státy tváří v tvář rozpínavosti Čínské lidové republiky a ochránit dlouhodobé zájmy Washingtonu v oblasti. „Pivot" od začátku vyvolával rozporuplné reakce, jak v samotné Asii, kde u některých zemí vzbudil vysoká očekávání zatímco v Pekingu spíše obavy, tak v Evropě, která se obávala ztráty zájmu USA o NATO a bezpečnostní situaci na starém kontinentě. Téměř pět let od ohlášení „pivotu" se ukazuje, že tyto obavy byly do značné míry neopodstatněné. Došlo sice k posílení vojenské přítomnosti USA v oblasti, nicméně Obamova administrativa se i nadále snaží vyhnout konfliktu s Čínou a hledá spíše pokojná řešení problémů mezi Pekingem a dalšími zeměmi (zejména teritoriálních sporů v Jihočínském moři). Asi nejvýraznějším aspektem „pivotu" je tzv. Trans-Pacific Partnership, zóna volného obchodu mezi 12 zeměmi, které zahrnují i původně spíše skeptické Japonsko, ale nepatří k nim Čína. Jednání o dosažení dohody o závěrečném textu TPP byla zdlouhavá a komplikovaná a byla ukončena teprve v říjnu 2015. Nyní jej čeká ještě náročnější proces ratifikace v jednotlivých členských státech, kde například v USA nemá TPP jednoznačnou podporu Kongresu. Jak je tedy patrné, „pivot" patrně nepřinesl tak zásadní změnu amerického angažmá v Asii a Tichomoří, jak někteří očekávali, a zároveň, s ohledem na dění ve východní Evropě a na Blízkém východě, ani výraznější ústup USA z těchto oblastí. Je však nutno mít na paměti, že je ještě stále příliš brzy komplexně hodnotit „pivot", neboť některé jeho dopady se projeví až v dlouhodobém horizontu.

Beatrix Balogh
US Citizenship of Overseas Territories

The essentially interdisciplinary discusses how the question of US citizenship shapes the political discourse in and about US Overseas Territories. These territories include such strategically located inhabited islands as Puerto Rico and Guam, and a number of other larger or smaller lands mostly scattered around in the Pacific. Partly due to their geographical and indeed geostrategic locations, statehood remains profoundly elusive for the territories today. Full-fledged, constitutional citizenship, nevertheless, is still perceived by Insular Americans as the crux of political integration. After a brief overview of the main features of Insular Citizenship and the milestones of its acquisition the paper will focus on recent trends and events that can potentially transform the citizenship debate from an academic question to an agenda-setting issue. The paper will identify research areas that are affected by a recent application of the infamous *Insular Cases*, and will also highlight how a US veteran's complaints about not being able to vote for a President may gain attention in the upcoming presidential elections.

Az USA politikai rendszerének minden pozitívuma és az intézmények hatékony működése mellett létezik az amerikai állampolgárságnak egy olyan formája, amely névleg azonos, mégis „más" mint az alapértelmezett, az alkotmány 14. kiegészítése által védett intézmény. Nem a bevándorlók valamely átmeneti státusza ez, hanem az USA külterületeinek – magyar terminológiában: társult országok – állampolgáraié. Nem csak amerikai útlevéllel rendelkeznek, de szabadon letelepedhetnek és munkát vállalhatnak az USA bármely tagállamában, szolgálnak a hadseregben, tehát jogok és kötelességek egyaránt együtt járnak az állampolgárságukkal. A demokratikus deficit ugyanakkor két ponton szembetűnő: ezek az állampolgárok egyrészt nem vehetnek részt az elnökválasztásban, másrészt nem rendelkeznek teljes jogú képviselettel az USA törvényhozásában, a Kongresszusban. Ez a megosztottság – egyes szerzők szerint másodrangú állampolgárság – a széles nyilvánosság számára leginkább a hadseregben nagy számban szolgáló Puerto Ricói és a csendes óceániai szigetekről származó amerikaiak példáján keresztül válik kézzel fogható problémává. Időről-időre felmerül az igény a helyzet rendezésére, de épp a külterületek földrajzi, geopolitikai helyzete, illetve az USA-hoz fűződő politikai viszonya bizonyul a folyamat kerékkötőjének, míg az állampolgársági modell az elmúlt 250 évben változatlan maradt. A tanulmány az amerikai állampolgárság e sajátos változatának problematikáját tárgyalja, ennek összefüggésében kitér a történelmi előzményekre, és bemutatja, hogyan befolyásolhatja a jogi formulák részleteibe menő vita a szigetek státuszát érintő politikai diskurzust.

Anna Bartnik
Illegal, Undocumented or Unauthorized. A Few Reflections on Unauthorized Population in the United States
Among the immigrant groups living in the USA there is a numerous group consisting of those residing without authorization. Estimates say

there are about 11 million unauthorized immigrants in the US. The main purpose of this article is to show certain issues connected with the presence of unauthorized immigrants in the US and present the basic, most recent trends in illegal immigration. The article also focuses on differences between words or phrases used to describe the unauthorized immigrant population.

Wśród imigrantów mieszkających w USA liczną grupę stanowią ci, którzy przebywają tam bezprawnie. Szacunkowe dane wskazują, że ich liczba przekroczyła już 11 milionów. Głównym celem artykułu jest przybliżenie kilku ogólnych refleksji związanych z zagadnieniem nielegalnej imigracji w USA, w tym m.in. problemów z właściwą terminologią opisującą populację nieautoryzowanych imigrantów.

Emőke Horváth
The Departure of the Covadonga. The Catholic Clergy after the Triumph of the Cuban Revolution (1960-1961)
In her contribution, Emőke Horváth focuses on the relationship between the Cuban Catholic Church and the State after the victory of the Revolution in 1960-1962. The author seeks answers to how the relation of the state toward the Church changed, and what role was played by the Cuban Primate, Pérez Serantes, and the Cuban prelates. She analyzes the political-economic measures that have shaped and influenced Church-State relations and she endeavors to reveal the factors that compelled one hundred and thirty-one priests to leave Cuba at the same time, in September 1961.

A tanulmány a kubai katolikus egyház és az állam viszonyát elemzi közvetlenül a forradalom győzelmét követően, az 1960-1962 közötti időszakban. Arra keresi a szerző a választ, hogy hogyan változott meg a hatalom viszonya a katolikus egyház irányába, ebben milyen mértékben játszott szerepet a kubai prímás, Enrique Pérez Serantes, valamint általában a felsőpapság tevékenysége. Végig veszi azokat a politikai-gazdasági intézkedéseket, melyek kihatottak az egyházra és formálták az államhoz fűződő viszonyát, igyekszik rámutatni azokra a főbb csomópontokra, melyek Castro és a hatalom egyre élesebb egyházellenességét jelezték, míg végül 1961 szeptemberében a kubai papság egy jelentős hányadát az ország elhagyására kényszerítették.

William R. Glass
Justifying American Interventionism: The 'Americans in Mexico' Westerns of the 1950s and 1960s

A subgenre of westerns I call "Americans in Mexico westerns" of the first two decades of the Cold War reveals a growing disillusionment with an activist foreign policy of intervention designed to promote independence and economic development. The films of the 1950s and early 1960s expressed the popular sentiment that US foreign policy should support the aspirations of people to find self-determination by freeing themselves from oppressive, exploitive dictators or governments. Then, beginning in the mid-1960s, some of these movies offered a darker, more cynical commentary on US foreign policy. These films reflected the growing doubts about the Cold War consensus and the ability of the United States to promote and defend democracy abroad in the name of containing communism. This evolution can be seen by looking at three representative films of this genre: *The Magnificent Seven* (1960), *The Professionals* (1966), and *The Wild Bunch* (1969).

Westerny nazwane przeze mnie westernami „Amerykanie w Meksyku" stanowią grupę filmów powstałych w pierwszych dwóch dekadach zimnej wojny, które pokazują rosnące rozczarowanie aktywną polityką zagranicznych interwencji w celu wspierania niepodległości i rozwoju ekonomicznego. Filmy z lat 50. i wczesnych lat 60. XX wieku wyrażały powszechne odczucia, że polityka zagraniczna USA powinna wspierać aspiracje narodów do samostanowienia poprzez uwolnienie się od opresji i wyzysku ze strony dyktatorów lub rządów. Później jednak, poczynając od połowy lat 60., niektóre z tych filmów zaczęły w sposób o wiele bardziej pesymistyczny i cyniczny komentować amerykańską politykę zagraniczną. Tę ewolucję postaw można prześledzić na podstawie trzech reprezentatywnych filmów tego gatunku: *The Magnificent Seven* (*Siedmiu wspaniałych*) z roku 1960, *The Professionals* (1966), i *The Wild Bunch* (*Dzika banda*) z roku 1969.

Krisztina Magyar
Womb and Breasts: Female Body Parts in Seventeenth-Century Puritan Political Communications

This paper will explore conceptualization of the Church of England as mother in four documents compiled in the 1630s by two eminent Puritan divines, John Cotton and Richard Mather. More narrowly, the paper will examine use of a biblical synecdoche, that of the womb and breasts, in the documents in question, all of which were composed in a historical period that saw large numbers of Puritans leave their homeland and settle in the New World. The paper will show that although use of the trope reflects Calvin's understanding of the institutional church as a mother who both gives birth to and nourishes believers, when inserted into political communications relating to the New England experiment during the 1630s, the trope comes to carry additional meaning.

A tanulmány transzatlanti perspektívából vizsgálja az amerikai történelem kezdeti éveit, amihez négy, az 1630-as években keletkezett puritán dokumentumot hív segítségül. A tárgyalt dokumentumok mindegyike kényes kérdést érint: az Újvilágba kivándorló angol puritánoknak az anglikán egyházhoz fűződő további viszonyát. A tanulmány azt mutatja be, hogy Kálvin anyametaforája, melyet az egyházra alkalmazott, és amely a vizsgált dokumentumok mindegyikében fellelhető, hogyan telítődik további jelentéssel az első generációs újvilági puritánok történelmi tapasztalatában.

Irén Annus
From Mollywood with Humor: A Mormon Pride and Prejudice

One of the most successful musicals of recent years is *The Book of Mormon* (2012), a work that fits into a series of mainstream American productions that have drawn on Mormon characters as their source of humor. At the same time, the emerging Mormon film industry (Mollywood) has also been producing a number of contemporary comedies about Mormons and their culture. While these tend to be low-budget films with certain attendant shortcomings, they demonstrate a refreshingly new self-reflective criticism of Latter-day culture through the humor they employ in both storyline and characterization.

This study takes a closer look at one of the classic examples of these movies, a Jane Austen adaptation entitled *Pride and Prejudice: A Latter-day Comedy* (2003) and explores the role of the humor through which the film presents and challenges Mormonism. It argues that the movie uses a special brand of humor in intersecting Austen's figures and situations with those typical of Mormonism, thus offering a form of entertainment that would encourage a Mormon audience to contemplate its own culture and associated stereotypes. However, the humor has been applied with sensitivity, and thus the movie does not offend the LDS culture, which is also the filmmaker's own. The paper proposes that, in a broader context, the film captures the spirit of Mollywood comedies, signifying that Mormon culture has come of age as a powerful, self-assured and stable subculture that is sufficiently comfortable viewing itself with laughter, but avoiding the moral concern that would arise from a sense of mockery or disloyalty to faith and community.

Habár a humor elismerten fontos szerepet játszik a társadalomban, számos tanulmány foglalkozik a humor és vallás között fennálló „történelmi bizalmatlansággal". Ezért az ön-reflexív humor megjelenése adott vallási csoporton belül izgalmas jelenség, ami joggal állhat tudományos vizsgáló-dások középpontjában. Jelen dolgozat egy jól ismert mollywoodi komédia, a Jane Austen regényének feldolgozásából készült Büszkeség és balítélet: Utolsó-napi komédia (2003) című filmet teszi elemzése tárgyául. A tanulmány bemutatja, a film hogyan fordul a különböző mormon sztereotípiák felé egy újszerű ön-reflexív kritikai humorral, olyan helyzeteket teremtve, melyek a nézőket saját kultúrájuk átgondolására késztetik – megbántás nélkül. A szerző amellett érvel, hogy szélesebb értelemben a mollywoodi vígjátékok azt jelzik, hogy a mormon kultúra érett, magabiztos és erős szubkultúrává nőtt, ami immár feszélyezettség és megbántódás nélkül tudja önmagát: hitét és társadalmi helyét a humor eszközein keresztül szemlélni.

Orsolya Anna Sudár
Memory Forgotten: the Importance of Narrative in Collective Memory Through Two Case Studies

Urban theory has long agreed that the formation of memory in cities is founded on the condition that memories in effect take up space: in the form of a memorial, monument or even just a plaque. Aldo Rossi's city remembers through its buildings, Walter Benjamin or Marcel Proust's city is a montage of infinite subjective memories and traces. In the case of memorial sites it is the demarcation of space that allows for the act of remembering, however, in many other cases this demarcation does not occur. This paper seeks to pinpoint where the sites of memory, as in Pierre Nora's *lieux de mémoire*, do not present themselves in the detectable realms of the city but occur in narrative texts such as photographs, or they are found in a network of cited but unconnected memories of the past and eventually realize themselves as "precedents" through posterior knowledge.

The paper also considers the way expectations of urban disaster are inscribed in narratives of tragedy and, setting two typically American case studies at aim, it wishes to understand the relation between the visual documentation, representation and expectation of urban trauma. The two case studies presented here are the Triangle Shirtwaist Factory fire of 1911 and the first bombing of Wall Street on September 16, 1920.

Az urbanisztikában általánosan elfogadott az az elképzelés, hogy az emlék megformálásához fizikai térre van szükség: emlékműre, műemlékre, plakettre. Az Alberto Rossi által leírt tökéletes város az épületein keresztül emlékezik meg múltjáról; a benjamini és proust-i rendszerben a város végtelen számú személyes emlék és emléknyom őrzőhelye. Míg a hagyományos emlékezőhelyek esetében a múlt felidézése a tér e célra való kijelölésének gesztusán keresztül valósul meg, sok másik esetben ez a gesztus nem valósul meg, vagy épp nem tud megvalósulni. Ez a tanulmány olyan emlékezőhelyeket kíván bemutatni, melyek esetében a Pierre Nora által definiált *lieu de mémoire* nem a fizikai szférában mutatkozik meg. A New York-i Triangle ruhagyár 1911-es tűzeseténél készült fotók és a Wall Street 1920-as bombatámadása két olyan példa, ahol a kollektív emlékezet a térbeli helyfoglalás helyett olyan narrált textusokban mutatkozik meg, melyek akárcsak a fotó, idézet tárgyává válnak, és melyek új kollektív élmények hatására a történelemből kiemelt precedens-történetekké válnak. E két tanulmányeset fölveti azt a kérdést is, hogy miként befolyásolja egy városi katasztrófa kollektív feldolgozását annak dokumentációja, reprezentációja és a katasztrófa beköveztéről előzetesen alkotott, a kollektív tudattalanban keringő fantáziakép.

Ivan Lacko
(Re)dramatizing, (Re)framing and (Re)writing History in Suzan-Lori Parks' The America Play

In an interview, Suzan-Lori Parks stated that when conceiving *The America Play* her intent was "to write about a hole" in American history, a hole that came to represent the void in the African American construction of identity brought about by negating white influence in history making and interpretation. Drawing on Henry Louis Gates's notion of "signifying meaning" in literary (and other) texts, this paper seeks to present and analyze the approach Suzan-Lori Parks takes in *The America Play* to challenge the framing of African American history, culture, politics and language, as well as to discuss the intricacies of the consequent reframing of these terms. Combining a critical examination of text and performance, I intend to consider the importance of absence, or "a hole" (or, in this particular context "the Great Hole of History") in the process of (re)-claiming cultural identity, and also to analyze the context of the process which Deborah Geis refers to as "rewriting [iconic characters] through the prism of African American cultural history".

Suzan-Lori Parks v jednom z rozhovorov uviedla, že pri písaní svojej hry *The America Play* chcela písať "o diere v amerických dejinách", o akomsi chýbajúcom mieste v afroamerickej konštrukcii identity, ktoré vzniklo negovaním väčšinového bieleho vplyvu v procese vytvárania a interpretácie dejín. Vychádzajúc z Henry Louis Gatesovej myšlienky o "signifikovaní významu" v (nielen) literárnych textoch, tento príspevok si kladie za cieľ odprezentovať a zanalyzovať Parksovej prístup v hre *The America Play*, pomocou ktorého spochybňuje rámcovú definíciu afroamerických dejín, kultúry, politiky a jazyka, a ktorý jej následne pomáha predefinovať význam týchto termínov. Spojením kritickej analýzy textu a inscenačného naštudovania hry chcem pojednať o dôležitosti absencie, alebo "diery" (resp. toho čo Parksová nazýva "Veľkou Dierou v Dejinách"), v priebehu (opätovného) hľadania a nárokovania si na kultúrnu identitu. Takisto chcem analyzovať širší kontext procesu, ktorý Deborah Geisová pomenovala ako "prepisovanie [ikonických postáv] cez prizmu afroamerických kultúrnych dejín".

Contributors

Irén Annus is an Associate Professor of American Studies at the University of Szeged in Hungary. Her research interest has focused on Identity Studies, more specifically the social construction and visual representation of minority groups in the last two centuries, based on gender, race/ethnicity and religion in the US. She has lectured and published extensively in these areas, both in Hungary and abroad.

Beatrix Balogh. Forsaking a previous career in Business Communication and Consultancy in favor of pursuing her academic interests, Beatrix Balogh began research on the Political Status and Citizenship of US Overseas territories in 2004. She earned an MA in American Studies and TESOL from ELTE University in 2007. She is currently a PhD candidate at Eötvös Loránd University's American Studies Program and works as a Lecturer at Károli Gáspár University offering a wide range of courses.

Anna Bartnik earned her Ph.D. degree in the Institute of Political Science at Jagiellonian University, in Cracow, Poland. Since then she has been working as Assistant Professor at the Jagiellonian University in the Institute of American Studies and Polish Diaspora. Her research concerns studies on American immigration law, Hispanic immigrants in the USA and local government in the US. She has published articles on subjects related to her research and a book *Latino Immigrants in the United States after World War II. Cubans, Mexicans and Puerto Ricans.*

Jan Bečka, Ph.D., currently works at the Ministry of Defence of the Czech Republic, where he focuses, among other things, on the US foreign and security policy. Previously he taught at the Faculty of Social Sciences, Charles University in Prague, where he specialized in current security and political developments in the world and American history (with the emphasis on the US policy towards Asia-Pacific). In 2014, he was deployed to Kosovo and worked in the Office of the Chief Political Advisor to the Commander of the NATO Kosovo Force (KFOR) mission.

Réka M. Cristian is an Associate Professor and Chair of the American Studies Department, University of Szeged. She is author of *Cultural Vistas and Sites of Identity: Literature, Film and American Studies* (2011), co-author (with Zoltán Dragon) of *Encounters of the Filmic Kind: Guidebook to Film Theories* (2008) and general editor of AMERICANA E-Journal of American Studies in Hungary and its e-book division, AMERICANA eBooks.

William R. Glass is Professor of American Social History at the American Studies Center of the University of Warsaw, Poland, where he is also co-editor of *The Americanist*, the journal published by the Center. He has published articles on American Protestant fundamentalism and a book entitled *Strangers in Zion: Fundamentalism in the South, 1900-1950*. He is currently working on a book tentatively titled "Laughing in War/Laughing at War: the Service Comedy as Genre".

Ewelina Gutowska-Kozielska, Ph.D., Institute of English and American Studies University of Gdańsk, Research Interests: American culture and politics, media, rhetoric, power and ideolosm, feminism & women studies, language and gender, sociolinguistics.

Emőke Horváth is a historian, a Hispanist, an Associate Professor at the University of Miskolc. She earned her M.A. and Ph.D. from the University of Budapest (ELTE, History and Hispanic Studies). Her researches focus on two main topics: 1. The Early Medieval Church history of the Iberian Peninsula, 2. The Church-State relations in Latin-America; the history of Cuban Revolution, and recently started to deal with the problems of Caribbean Identity. She participated in European history networks (2005-2010), e.g. Cliohresnet, the Network of Excellence. She has organized several conferences, has published books and articles on medieval and Latin American history.

Maxim Kucer is a Ph.D. candidate at the Department of American Studies, Faculty of Social Scienceses at Charles University in Prague. His research interest includes the populist movement in the 19th century America, the Tea Party movement, and US foreign policy in Asia.

Ivan Lacko is an Assistant Professor at the Department of English and American Studies, Faculty of Arts, Comenius University in Bratislava, Slovakia. His academic interests include theater, American studies and literature, cultural studies, and creative writing. He has had extensive experience with theater as a practitioner, playwright and director. In 2012, as a Fulbright scholar, he did research at the University of Minnesota focusing on community-based theatre in the United States. At present, he is extending this research to the social and political role of new theatre in Central Europe – with a specific focus on its impact on social awareness, critical literacy, and political engagement.

Krisztina Magyar owns master's degrees in French and English language and literature, which she obtained from Eötvös Loránd University, Budapest, in 1994 and 1996, respectively. Since her graduation, Krisztina has been working as a language teacher at secondary school level. At present she is also working toward a Ph.D. in American Studies at Eötvös Loránd University. In general, she is interested in the relationship between religion and American culture. Her dissertation project is a cognitive linguistic investigation of Christian nonviolence in the thought of Martin Luther King, Jr. Krisztina is also fascinated by Puritanism, especially the movement's earliest years in America.

Agnieszka Małek is an Assistant Professor and Vice-Director for student affairs at the Institute of American Studies and Polish Diaspora of the Jagiellonian University. She earned her Ph.D. from the Institute of Sociology at the Jagiellonian University. Her research and teaching interests include migration and mobility, migration policy, Italian diaspora in the New World and qualitative research methods.

Peter Rusiňák is the co-founder of the Center for North American Studies (CNAS) at the University of Economics in Bratislava, where he currently holds a position of the Executive Director.

Radosław Rybkowski is the Associate Professor and Director of the Institute of American Studies and Polish Diaspora of the Jagiellonian University in Krakow. His fields of interest include: American theatre and musicals; the development of American civilization and most of all – the US and Canadian higher education policy. During the spring semester of 2009 he was the Fulbright visiting scholar at the Steinhardt School of Culture, Education and Human Development of the New York University. He is currently teaching courses in the history of North American Civilization; American Musical, focusing on perception of this theatrical genre; and in the history of American theatre. He has published articles on American theatre as well as on the higher education policy, including two books on US higher education system.

Orsolya Anna Sudár is currently a doctoral student of Eötvös Loránd University in Budapest, Hungary. Her research is mainly concerned with visual culture and literature; her research mainly discussed the relationship between urban design, architecture and collective memory. The domains of cultural studies and American studies intersect in her analyses, in which New York serves as a recurring case in point. She is writing her dissertation on the issue of urban authenticity and narratives of tragedy inscribed into the texture of the city.

Index